I0420570

Editor-in-Chief and Founder:
 Lyndon H. LaRouche, Jr.
Editorial Board: *Lyndon H. LaRouche, Jr. , Helga
 Zepp-LaRouche, Paul Gallagher, Tony Papert,
 Gerald Rose, Dennis Small, Jeffrey Steinberg,
 William Wertz*
Co-Editors: *Paul Gallagher, Tony Papert*
Managing Editor: *Nancy Spannaus*
Technology: *Marsha Freeman*
Books: *Katherine Notley*
Ebooks: *Richard Burden*
Graphics: *Alan Yue*
Photos: *Stuart Lewis*
Circulation Manager: *Stanley Ezrol*

INTELLIGENCE DIRECTORS
Counterintelligence: *Jeffrey Steinberg, Michele
 Steinberg*
Economics: *John Hoefle, Marcia Merry Baker,
 Paul Gallagher*
History: *Anton Chaitkin*
Ibero-America: *Dennis Small*
Russia and Eastern Europe: *Rachel Douglas*
United States: *Debra Freeman*

INTERNATIONAL BUREAUS
Bogotá: *Miriam Redondo*
Berlin: *Rainer Apel*
Copenhagen: *Tom Gillesberg*
Houston: *Harley Schlanger*
Lima: *Sara Madueño*
Melbourne: *Robert Barwick*
Mexico City: *Gerardo Castilleja Chávez*
New Delhi: *Ramtanu Maitra*
Paris: *Christine Bierre*
Stockholm: *Ulf Sandmark*
United Nations, N.Y.C.: *Leni Rubinstein*
Washington, D.C.: *William Jones*
Wiesbaden: *Göran Haglund*

ON THE WEB
e-mail: eirns@larouchepub.com
www.larouchepub.com
www.executiveintelligencereview.com
www.larouchepub.com/eiw
Webmaster: *John Sigerson*
Assistant Webmaster: *George Hollis*
Editor, Arabic-language edition: *Hussein Askary*

EIR (ISSN 0273-6314) *is published weekly
(50 issues), by EIR News Service, Inc.,
P.O. Box 17390, Washington, D.C. 20041-0390.
(703) 777-9451*

European Headquarters: E.I.R. GmbH, Postfach
Bahnstrasse 9a, D-65205, Wiesbaden, Germany
Tel: 49-611-73650
Homepage: http://www.eirna.com
e-mail: eirna@eirna.com
Director: Georg Neudecker

Montreal, Canada: 514-461-1557

Denmark: EIR - Danmark, Sankt Knuds Vej 11,
basement left, DK-1903 Frederiksberg, Denmark.
Tel.: +45 35 43 60 40, Fax: +45 35 43 87 57. e-mail:
eirdk@hotmail.com.

Mexico City: EIR, Sor Juana Inés de la Cruz 242-2
Col. Agricultura C.P. 11360
Delegación M. Hidalgo, México D.F.
Tel. (5525) 5318-2301
eirmexico@gmail.com

Canada Post Publication Sales Agreement
#40683579

Postmaster: Send all address changes to *EIR*, P.O.
Box 17390, Washington, D.C. 20041-0390.

Signed articles in *EIR* represent the views of the
authors, and not necessarily those of the Editorial
Board.

History Is Being Made In Manhattan

The Great Cookie-Cutter in the Sky

by Tony Papert

Sept. 12—Let me tell you about some of the most important articles you won't be reading in this issue of *EIR*. One is an in-depth discussion of the 1962 Cuban Missile Crisis. (We've had two recent articles on this by Jeffrey Steinberg, but this one was to be a more in-depth study by the same author.) I proposed this article to Editor-in-Chief Lyndon LaRouche on Sept. 10. My motivation was that a leading Democrat had just commented privately, after Russian President Putin's surprise move into Syria, to the effect that it appeared to him that the United States might be heading into something like a new Cuban Missile Crisis,—but without a John Kennedy in the White House. Anything but.

LaRouche shot it down instantly. "No," he said, "we shouldn't do that. This is *not* a new Cuban Missile Crisis. I don't know what it is, but it's definitely not a new Cuban Missile Crisis."

Okay.

Another idea which I had also drawn up and had just discussed with Editorial Board members, was a juxtaposition of Lyndon LaRouche's contemporaneous understanding of the critical, turning-point importance of Russia's two Chechen Wars in the 1990s, with Putin's vivid understanding of the existential importance of the Second Chechen War at just the same moment.

"No," said LaRouche. "This is not anything like a continuation of the Chechen Wars. There's a relationship, but it's completely different."

All right. He went on to reject yet a third proposed article on analogous grounds. (Although he enthusiastically endorsed the other articles which appear here.)

I put down the phone in a gloomy and irritated state. I knew that I had been wrong,—but how? What did it mean? Then, the moment he finished his editorial discussion with me, LaRouche began his nationwide Fireside Chat with supporters around the U.S. I found it extremely thought-provoking. But throughout that call-in program, and then overnight and into the early morning, I wrestled with myself over the significance of that earlier discussion.

What had just happened?

Putin had suddenly outflanked Obama, to Obama's complete surprise and astonishment. Obama had been attacking Putin in Europe, centering on Ukraine; he had thought he was succeeding. Suddenly, Putin shows up and attacks Obama unexpectedly from the rear, from the Middle East, by threatening to destroy the ISIS terrorists. As part of the same flanking action, Putin had influenced China's organization of its unprecedented and brilliant military display at its September 3, Seventieth Anniversary Victory Day celebrations, with Putin their number one guest.

Simultaneously,—and neither coincidentally nor in any simple relationship,—Europe had suddenly begun to break away from the British-Obama dictatorship which had aligned all the Europeans for near-term thermonuclear war against Russia, while locking them into the anti-Russian sanctions policy which was shutting down German industry. The initial breakaway came, again, from a completely unexpected direction: Germany reversed itself on the question of the floods of refugees from Obama's disastrous wars. Suddenly, the German government reversed itself and committed to accept 800,000 to a million refugees this year, and half a million each subsequent year. Just at that moment, the anti-Blairite Jeremy Corbyn was elected leader of the British Labour Party in a landslide victory. Then, the German Foreign Ministry said it welcomes Russian participation in the fight against ISIS in Syria. German Chancellor Merkel was quoted to say that the Germans, along with other Europeans, want Russia to be involved in solving the Syria war,—while meanwhile, Obama's White House continued to struggle internally over how to respond. Signs come from France; other possible signs from Italy.

This is an historic, once-in-a-lifetime opportunity,—but exactly what is it? Well, the fact is, in reality, we just don't yet fully know what it is. We don't know, but we have the duty to learn what it is,—in the course of exploiting the opportunity it offers us to avert an imminent thermonuclear war by turning Obama out of the White House, and cancelling the bankrupt Wall Street system.

But we know what it is *not*. It certainly is not,—as Lyndon LaRouche told me Thursday night,—it is not a new Cuban Missile Crisis. It is not a continuation of the Chechen Wars. More generally, it is not a *revenant*, a ghost, a corpse of the undead returning from past history like last night's pizza.

Exactly the opposite. This is totally new. It is *sui generis*, or, in English, "one of a kind."

And right now, if there is any one sure recipe for defeat, in this unique, all-embracing crisis which opens up the path towards victory, it is just that,—to imagine that we are living through a repeat of past history, when in fact, just the opposite is true. What is going on now is totally new and unprecedented.

The Duty to Learn

With this, I was reminded again of one of the most inspiring books I have ever read: the autobiography of

Lt. Gen. Vasily Chuikov, commander at the Battle of Stalingrad, 1943.

Soviet Marshal Vasily Ivanovich Chuikov, *The Beginning of the Road*. Stalingrad was the "beginning of the road" towards the defeat of Hitler and the Nazis; it was the turning point of the whole war, and likewise one of the greatest victories of the human spirit amidst the great darkness of the Twentieth Century. Chuikov and his ever-dwindling 62nd Soviet Army had held the city for 100 days against von Paulus' Sixth Army, and against the Luftwaffe's total control of the air. By the end, the 62nd was hanging on to no more than a square kilometer or less, but it was that square kilometer,—like Kepler's eight minutes of arc,—which permitted the great encircling operation which finally

House-to-house fighting in the Stalingrad suburbs.

turned the tide of World War II.

When he had been ordered back to European Russia from Asia, the long train ride had given Chuikov time to think. "What is this new system of war which the Germans are using, which defeats us in almost every en-

Frontline clashes in an urban area of Syria, May 2015.

gagement? Just exactly what is it they're doing, and how can we counter it?" Once he arrived at the front, Chuikov spent a lot of time in solo reconnaissance from hilltops, which will remind our readers of Douglas MacArthur in World War I.

He observed the carefully choreographed advances of the Germans wedging themselves over and through the weaker positions in the Russian lines. First came the Luftwaffe, followed by combined formations of tanks and infantry. "I wonder if I can get them to bomb their own troops?" he asked himself. He tested it out. Shortly before the German attack was to come, Russian troops under his command quickly evacuated their own trenches, and in effect invited the Germans in. Along comes the Luftwaffe, and bombs their own German troops, just as he expected. The German soldiers fired off rockets to try to warn off their planes, but to no avail.

Skipping briefly over Chuikov's whole enthralling account, as we are forced to do here for reasons of space, we can link these first observations and experiments of his, to one of the tactics he made famous, called "hugging the enemy." Where possible (or impossible), Chuikov's troops placed their lines so close to the enemy, practically in his lap, that German air supe-

riority often became semi-useless; it could not be exercised for fear of inadvertently hitting German positions.

Then, when he was given the order to defend Stalingrad at all costs, Chuikov invented an entirely new method of warfare for the battle in the now-destroyed city. As he wrote, nothing like this was ever taught in military academies; indeed, it had never even been dreamed of before. Others called it "street warfare," but, as Chuikov wrote, you never wanted to be caught in a street in Stalingrad; you'd be obliterated. Much of the fighting consisted of seizing fortified buildings, left standing amidst the rubble, from the enemy at night. Chuikov re-formed whole units down into 21-man squads, subdivided into specialized groups, which seized the buildings, and often cleared them hall by hall, and room by room.

And as in war, to think you understand this current, September 2015 crisis by analogy with past events, is to be deluded, to know less then nothing at all, and is tantamount to instant, disastrous defeat.

Now, Lyndon LaRouche has long emphasized the harmfulness of mathematics for science, i.e., for understanding the truth, especially since British Lord Bertrand Russell contrived to substitute mathematics for science at the beginning of the Twentieth Century, and to hound and persecute actual scientists, most prominently Albert Einstein, who refused to go along with this fraud. But what is the issue? The issue is precisely the same. The mathematical mind, as Edgar Allan Poe argued tirelessly in his time, is the mind which believes that everything is known, everything has been discovered, and there is nothing that is truly new; at most, anything which might appear to be new, can simply be deduced from the same tired old axioms.

It is the mind of the sucker, of the born loser.

EIR Contents

www.larouchepub.com Volume 42, Number 37, September 18, 2015

UN/Milton Grant

Cover This Week

A view of the United Nations headquarters in Manhattan

History Is Being Made In Manhattan

2 EDITORIAL
The Great Cookie-Cutter in the Sky
by Tony Papert

6 Creating a Peace Paradigm: A New Era For Mankind Where We All Become Truly Human
The opening presentations by Lyndon LaRouche, former Attorney General Ramsey Clark, former U.S. Senator Mike Gravel (Alaska), and Helga Zepp-LaRouche at the Manhattan conference on Sept. 12.

18 Dialogue: It is Feasible to Dump Obama and End This Plan of War

41 Unsolved Mysteries of the Atomic Nucleus: A Universe in the very small
by Liona Fan-Chiang
In relatively low-energy domains, below the level of sub-atomic particles, there are still many outstanding paradoxes, some almost a millennium old.

45 Iran's Contributions to World Fusion Research Poised for Take-Off
by Marsha Freeman
Featuring an exclusive interview with Iranian fusion scientist Dr. Mahmood Ghoranneviss

47 Ten Years of Progress in Iran Tokamak Diagnostic Upgrades

49 The Role of Wilhelm Furtwängler In the New Paradigm for Peace: The New Eurasian Landbridge
by Mindy Pechenuk, with Megan Beets

54 Furtwängler's Nemesis Supported Bertrand Russell

A New Era For Mankind Where We All Become Truly Human

Lyndon LaRouche, former Attorney General Ramsey Clark, former U.S. Senator Mike Gravel (Alaska), and Helga Zepp-LaRouche keynoted the Manhattan Project conference on Sept. 12.

Dennis Speed: My name is Dennis Speed, and on behalf of the Schiller Institute, I'd like to welcome you to today's conference: "Creating a Peace Paradigm: A New Era for Mankind Where We All Become Truly Human." Our format today is that we're going to have a symposium, and we're going to begin right away with our first speaker, the Founding Editor of *Executive Intelligence Review*, the economist and statesman whom you all know, most people love, and some people are scared as Hell of, Lyndon LaRouche. [applause]

Lyndon H. LaRouche

Lyndon LaRouche: I'm particularly relieved that I've had another chance to meet with our dear friend here, and I'm really honored by his appearance here at this time.

The issue before us, is one of the most momentous in modern history, and probably history in general. We're on the verge of a general thermonuclear war on a global scale. That does not mean that this is necessarily going to happen, but it means the actions we're going to have to take in order to prevent that from happening, are very strenuous and also urgent.

Now, we in the United States have the opportunity to present the case for this situation. The problem is—well, let me put it this way; I have time considerations, I'll add to this later.

But at the end of this week and the beginning of next week, one of the most momentous developments in all modern history is about to unfold. It's

UN/Milton Grant

In his address to the Schiller Conference, over video hookup, Lyndon LaRouche pointed to the upcoming UN General Assembly as "one of the most momentous developments in all modern history about to unfold."

going to unfold underneath this new assembly of the international movement of peace [at the United Nations General Assembly], which is the best term to call it. And so from that point on, we have to realize that that's the case. We are at the threshold of thermonuclear war. The President of the United States Obama is one of the principal instruments leading the world toward a thermonuclear war, and this means generally an extinction form of war.

This thing which is going to happen at the beginning of this next week, is probably absolutely necessary to avoid the danger of thermonuclear war. Now, of course, our President is the key source, the greatest source, of that threat right now. He's not as an individual, but as an individual as President of the United States. Unless he were suspended under the rules of the Twenty-Fifth Amendment, he could still set off a thermonuclear war on a global scale. All the potential for that exists now. And therefore, what is going to happen in the next week, the coming week, and henceforth in that period, is going to determine whether or not the world is ready to prevent the launching of a thermonuclear war. That's what the issue is.

There are many aspects to this. The question is, why did mankind ever let itself get involved into this kind of mess? Well, there were problems, faults, in the way people thought. For example, since the beginning of the Twentieth Century, our very system of life has become more and more degenerate. People are not quite as smart, or quite as concerned about humanity, as they were at the end of the preceding Century. And therefore, this is an urgent issue. We have to recognize that our school systems, our education system, our economic system as it's organized, our standards of living, our standards of education of our young people,—all of these things have been put into jeopardy since the beginning of the Twentieth Century, when this change occurred.

So now we've come to the point, where the Twentieth Century issue, has come to the point of the paymaster. *We must now take this moment* of this new international assembly, which is fully aware—its best people are aware—of the implications of this situation, now. And therefore, what we must organize around in the United States, in particular, but throughout the world, is to prevent the launching of a thermonuclear war. That's what Obama represents! And, to get him off the agenda, by the 25th Amendment, is the absolute requirement for the safety of mankind in general today.

Therefore, what was being assembled in the coming period, the international event, this event is absolutely crucial. It's also absolutely crucial that *we* contribute our abilities into making this next great convention successful. Because this may be the last chance for humanity. That's the extreme view, but things approximating that are there.

They have, however, been building up. Ever since Franklin Roosevelt left office, there has been, despite good Presidents—a few of them have occurred—despite those Presidents and other representatives of our government, the general characteristic of our government has been one of *degeneration*. Degeneration in everything; degeneration in respect to our Constitution, and its meaning. And therefore, this event, which is to be assembled in the coming week, is the thing on which we must all concentrate, not only inside the United States, but globally. There are movements in the world which can do this, but they have to be brought together, and the forces of a different disposition must be curtailed.

And, that's what I think the situation is, what I see, and what I fear.

Speed: OK. Very good. [applause]

Our next speaker is Ramsey Clark, former Attorney General of the United States. So, Ramsey, why don't you go right ahead, and respond as you will, to what you've just heard.

Ramsey Clark

Schiller Institute
Former U.S. Attorney General Ramsey Clark.

Clark: From here? I forgot I was wired! [laughter] I usually oppose wiring, but here I am, in front of all these people, wired. How good to see so many beautiful faces, who believe in the preparation, behind their faces, for struggle to overcome the human propensity toward self-destruction, war.

You know, when you think about our schoolchildren and all our babies, you realize that we still have this maniacal energy. Energy can be dangerous, as essential as it is to life, and the energy committed to destruction, to self-destruction; the billions we spend on the most sophisticated means of destroying big pieces of real estate, with lots of people on them; and even the pride that we take as a people in the capacity for self-destruction. Militarism ought to be the supreme crime, because it has been, and remains,—and because of its capacity for total destruction—ow more than ever, the greatest threat to life on Earth, and all the things that we can hope for, for our children, or, in my case, our great-grandchildren. Our materialism distracts us from, not only the best parts of life, those that really bring the most joy and happiness and satisfaction. But the clamor of our society, with technology in the driver's seat, and the driver is without a license.

When you think about militarism, think of Syria today: Damascus, beautiful Damascus, historic Damascus; a contender for, among half a dozen other places in the region, the oldest permanently settled place on Earth by human beings. It's been there for a long time; you don't have to be in the city but a few minutes before you're told about it, and it's a great story. But the threat to it, is much greater than any of the destructive potentials of history. The Roman troops were nothing compared what can happen today—the obliteration of whole cities with a single blast. And, somehow or other, we are able to live reasonably happily and normally, and not even think about it. And, when we do think about it, we think less of ourselves, because we can't find a way to do anything about it. We haven't found a way to do anything about it that's adequate to address the phenomenon.

Iraq, today, is a vast wasteland, as we used to say. The "cradle of civilization," in the Twenty-First Century a vast wasteland. You don't really want to go there. I have to go there; I've been going there too much for the last 20 years. Hasn't done any good, but we keep going, keep trying. With all that history, and all that love and all that knowledge, and all that violence that was mixed in with it, and finally, the violence seems to come out on top, doesn't it? Just staying alive in Iraq has been the principal challenge for every man, woman, and child that's living there. That may sound excessive, but go there and take a look. It's not just the constant threat of violence; it's where are you going to get potable water in the next days? And whether food will be available? And whether bombs will come down again?

And, still, rather than examine that, in acts of human unity and concern to change it, most of our energies and concentrations, on this subject, are devoted to more efficient means of mass destruction.

I'm an optimist, which has to mean, having said what I just said, a little crazy; but you have got to be crazy enough to face the situation, you know? A sane person would turn away from it.

And just look at the babies, and hug them. And there's more: what their future will be if we don't put our hearts and minds toward creating conditions, where there aren't millions constantly struggling to stay alive. Leaving their homelands, and going across wastelands and dangerous waters; and dying of thirst, and drowning on sinking boats. While we're wondering what the next Saturday afternoon movie will be at the theaters, a way of going away, of avoiding facing the reality of the condition of human conduct, and the life it's creating on a planet that in many areas is largely overcrowded, and doesn't seem to understand the possibility that that could create a problem; for all the organizations and mail we get about addressing the subject.

Our capacity to change all that is, to me, clear. It's a question of will. But we first have to have the will to face the facts, to organize and present the facts, in a way that every man, woman and child can see the havoc we're wreaking on this beautiful planet. A pretty terrific place to be born into, most of the centuries that we're aware of. There are scuffles around here and there that were cruel, and our species was the principal offender. But it's only in our time that making Mother Earth as lifeless as the Moon became a real possibility. We could scruff it up a little bit in the old days, but nothing serious. It's like walking through a rose garden, and getting scratched by a barb or two, here and there, a thorn.

Our capacity to overcome the problems we see, those that are risking their lives in boats to cross dangerous waters that they've never seen before, to try to get to a place where their feet could be dry, and their babies can be fed, and they can live in peace. It's clear, but we have to set our minds to it, and devote our energies to overcoming.

I'm a believer that energy is genius, and all that thinking doesn't change a thing until all that energy organizes and mobilizes it and moves it. And that's probably the main reason we're here today, is to see the problem, analyze the solution, and address it outright, and overcome.

So, I'll be anxious to hear your wisdom. Most of my

time is—like today, I have to go someplace else—I'll never get there in time. But I'll be with you in spirit, and I'll hear what was said later.

Best wishes to you, and our thanks to those who brought us together, Lyn. You're looking well, pal! I hope I'll see you, in person, around Christmastime. [applause]

Speed: Our next speaker, former U.S. Senator from Alaska; 2008 Presidential candidate; most notorious for his work back in the 1970s, concerning the infamous *Pentagon Papers*, Mike Gravel. [applause]

Mike Gravel

Mike Gravel: Thank you very much Dennis. Lyndon, I've got to say that you've got me by eight years, and what I've noticed in reading history, in the biographies of people like Arnold Toynbee and Will Durant (and of course his wife, but primarily Will) is that, as they got older in life, they became more pessimistic about the survival of the planet. And I must say that I'm an optimist, but I've got vestiges of this fear as I get older, that is there hope for the human race?

But what I'm really impressed with, is the work that you've done, Lyndon, your wife, the Schiller Institute, the *Executive Intelligence Review*, and this didn't come to be naturally, or quickly. I want to say that this lady up front here, Anita Gallagher, has been beating on me for a decade, and calls me. [laughter] And I got to tell you, I have been captured. I am now part of the team, and will work towards the goals.

I want to compliment you, and first off, let me say this: when you look to solutions, I wish I could say, as an American—because I love my country, and I'm sure all of you do, but I love the world more. When I was in the Senate, I used to get away with making extensive speeches, where I would end the speech that my priorities in life are first, the human race; second, the United States; and third, Alaska, and all my priorities are in that order.

And so all I can say now, is that I don't see a solution within the confines of the United States. I think that you're quite right in your assessment of the Obama Administration. But I've got to tell you that when you look to the Congress, and I can say when I was a Senator—you know, we had a certain arrogance, being Senators; we'd look to the House, and say, "Well, that's a zoo over there." But now, when I look from this distant po-

Schiller Institute
Former U.S. Senator from Alaska Mike Gravel.

sition, on the entire Congress, it is a *total zoo*, not just the House! And so, we focus on the Administration and the Presidency as the agent to work on. Well, I got to tell you, this other body is co-equal, and they can do things, and *have* been doing things, that have been *sabotaging—sabotaging*—and destroying *any* possibility we have for world peace.

So I've come to the conclusion, after a number of years, that I look elsewhere. I look to where the successes in life have been, of recent nature, and the attitudes. I want to compliment you, by underscoring what China is doing today. I personally feel that Putin is running his country a hell of a lot better than our last three or four Presidents have been running our country. [applause]

When you take the combination of the Chinese leadership—and I'll go into, in a moment, what they're doing, which is, I think, the *touchstone* of the Twenty-First Century. If [Henry] Luce wants to continue to hold the view that the last century was the American Century, I think it's not a good mark on our history, because it was a *terrible* century.

But now, when you look at the Twenty-First Century, who is the group that's actually acting in the most mature fashion, and has not made a reliance on military power? Of course, that's the problem with American foreign policy today. It's that, first, we think in terms of force, and use of our "superb" military. Well, one, they're not so superb; and two, it's *horrible* thinking. You can say that, well, the American people sustains this. Well, unfortunately, the American people, they're not stupid, but they are *totally* uninformed as to what's going on in the world today. Our six leading communications companies, which are total pawns of Wall Street, have guaranteed, that we will [audio loss] ....

What's going to happen, from my perspective? I don't disagree with your sense of urgency, don't disagree at all. But I've come to the conclusion that we could all be incinerated over the Kashmir, because any bombs going off between Pakistan and India will just wipe us out, too, in the process. It's the total human insanity we have, that we can deal and manipulate and control the bomb. We can't. Not at all. We're victims of circumstance.

Look to the Chinese

And so, when I take your views, they're as valid as mine. But my view is optimistic; I'm not old enough, yet, to be totally pessimistic. My view is that what China is doing, with the help of Russia, and with the BRICS, is really where the future of mankind lies, in terms of solutions. Not our leadership. It's going to be what they're [the Chinese] doing, and how they're handling it.

As I pointed out to you earlier, Putin has run things very well. After the provocation of Ukraine—and most Americans have forgotten that we're the ones that did this; we're the ones that did it. They don't hear that any more in the press. And I don't know if anybody has seen the recent "Frontline" piece on "Putin's Way": It was *horrible*. And I have an intelligence background.

When I was 23 years old. I was a top secret control officer. At 23, mind you. I was in Germany as an adjutant for a communications intelligence service. Our cover was the CIC. What did we do at this place? There were only two military officers—myself, 23, as a second lieutenant; and a lieutenant colonel, who was in the sauce a good part of the time. The rest of it was run by Germans. And what we did is, we'd open people's mail, wantonly, and wire-tap people in Europe, wantonly. Now, that's when I was 23 years old. [1953]

So you can figure, when we had the *Pentagon Papers* come up in the Senate, and a Senator could not go in and read the papers, except being under guard, couldn't take any notes; all I could think of was: when I was 23, I was acting with more power than any Senator can act right now in viewing the *Pentagon Papers*! So, little wonder that when Ellsberg approached me, and asked if I would read the *Pentagon Papers* as part of my filibuster against the draft, I said, instantaneously, "Of course, yes, I would!"

And so, now we come to the same situation that existed then and exists now: what the government, our government, is doing, is really what's leading the destruction throughout the world community. When you see the blow-back of these refugees, which we have not seen it at this level since the Second World War; when you see that going on right now—who's responsible for that? I would hope that, maybe, our European leaders, who are all wimps, led around by the American forces, both civilian and military, through NATO—which I want to characterize, as, NATO is the globalization of the military-industrial complex. That's what NATO is, and it's as useless as anything you could think of. We should dissolve NATO, first opportunity.

But let's get back to where the answers are, and what's going forward: it's what China is doing. And it's in their self-interest. There's nothing wrong with intelligent self-interest; and that's what they're exercising. Because they have overcapacity; they have a great deal of presence in the world—not military presence—but what they're going to do is to amass this into a force, to create the economic union, via communications and transportation systems, and general broad economic systems. They're going to go from western China to Europe, and then all the areas in-between. And this is going to give the world a focus of attention on *economic* solutions, rather than what we focus on now.

I was just listening to General [Michael] Flynn. A fine thing: The guy's admitting that they were doing things wrong, but not too much of an admission. But he was saying we failed, but the real answer is economic development in these areas, so that people could be concerned about their well-being and jobs in the future, rather than what they're doing now, which is annihilating themselves.

Well, this is exactly what China is putting forth, with the help of Russia, and tying it in. And *thank God* we have these institutions that are creating financial institutions to overcome the short-sightedness of the World Bank and IMF. So, they're leading in the financial area; they're leading in the economic area. And, if only we would have enough *sobriety* in this country to say, "Let's work with them."

Can you imagine? Since the Second World War, we have been the ascendant power in the world, and we've not acquitted ourselves very well. Look out at the world today, since the Second World War, and say, "This is nothing to be proud of." But what China is doing—and

Xinhua/Wang Ye

China's global expansion has been to build economic cooperation with nations around the globe. Here, Chinese Premier Li Keqiang meeting with South African Deputy President Cyril Ramaphosa in Beijing, July 14, 2015.

if we were to now say, "They're on the ascendancy, economically, and they're going to ride that horse to the saving of human civilization."

And so, here again, I want to compliment the La-Rouche organization for all that you're doing in this regard, in communicating this. And this is in line with views that I found out 20 years ago: I went to an event, as a normal citizen, to a LaRouche gathering, and that's when I became aware of what you wanted to do in crossing the Bering Sea into the Kamchatka Peninsula. And I was always fascinated by that as an Alaskan, because there's no question, it's very do-able.

I won't live, and you won't live, to see the fruits of what is going on today with this new wisdom exercised in China, in their leadership. Of course they're not falling prey to what we did. Their defense budget is 10% of our budget. And it's ridiculous that we feel such suspicion about what they're doing. But we've been on an ego trip for decades and decades, and all of a sudden, there's somebody coming forward that is going to eat our lunch, and we don't know how to stop them, because they're not talking about eating it with the force of arms. They're talking about outperforming us in an economic fashion.

And so, I just want to add my voice to the work that the *Executive Intelligence Review* is doing, what the Schiller Institute is doing, and say that *any* way I can help, I'm there. Because the opportunity is there—and, a little bit which is a take-off from your career, Lyndon— is that, if the truth be told, it is fully recognized by those who hear it, unfortunately. And you have a cadre of people who do hear it, who are committed to it, and now, count me as one of those aboard. Lyndon, thank you. And Helga, thank you for what you're doing. [applause]

Speed: Now we're going to hear the founder of the Schiller Institute, Helga La-Rouche. [applause]

Helga Zepp-LaRouche

Helga Zepp-LaRouche: Well, thank you. Thank you, Senator. Hello, Lyn!

When the Senator made his remarks, I reminded myself that when the Iraq War was conducted, we had a conference on the same day. And we were truly horrified. As a matter of fact, we knew that this was based on lies. The *EIR* had produced a report, half a year earlier, where we predicted that they would make this war, the Bush-Cheney-Blair combination. And we had tried to warn against it, because there were no weapons of mass destruction; there was no way that Saddam Hussein would have reached any city around the world in 45 minutes.

We knew it was a lie, and we published that in an *EIR* report, and we had distributed many leaflets around the world. And in Germany it led to a situation where in August, shortly before the war broke out, Gerhard Schröder all of a sudden made an about-face and said Germany is not going to participate in this war. And that had a very important influence in causing Jacques

Helga Zepp-LaRouche, with conference moderator Dennis Speed on her left.

Schiller Institute

10,000, 20,000 on the shores of the Greek islands; and the Greek Islands are poor, so the authorities have no food, they have no water, they have no medical supplies.

So, people are now trying to get to the mainland in Greece, and from there they are trying to get to Macedonia, which is exploding with refugees. People are trying to go further to Hungary, and there is a barbed wire wall built around Hungary. You saw these absolutely horrifying pictures, where you have small children caught between tear gas deployed by the police and refugees trying to get through these barbed wires. This is a breakdown of civilization, what is happening there; on top of all the other things which happened in Ukraine and other places. So, as a result, you have now an explosion of misery and refugees.

A Shift in Process

But something positive has happened. I think it remains to be seen what all went into it, but there was a sudden shift in the German policy. Now Mrs. Merkel, who I admit is not my favorite politician, responded to an impulse in the German population, where all of a sudden the German population who were pretty much in a soap bubble of unreality until very recently—because people in Germany behaved exactly like Americans, they said there's nothing you can do anyway. They felt completely impotent to change anything. As a matter of fact, this was not the American outlook some years ago, but in the recent period, Americans and Germans became pretty similar in their pessimism, but also indifferentism, not being interested in all these matters.

But suddenly—suddenly—people recognized, these poor people running away from war needed help. So you had an outpouring of love, of charity, people streaming by the thousands to the main rail stations in different cities, bringing clothes, bringing food, bringing necessities of life. I think it was that which caused Merkel to say, wait a second, the majority is going in

Chirac to also not go in this direction.

And so on that day when the war started, I was so horrified. I gave a speech at this conference and I just recalled that I said, are these people not aware that there is a higher law which will avenge this injustice? And I think I recalled the *Ibykus* poem by Friedrich Schiller; I said "Don't you know the lesson that if you commit a crime, there is such a thing as Erinyes, the goddesses of revenge which will come down on you?"

I think that that is exactly what we are seeing right now. Because one war followed the other one. You had the Iraq War. You had before that the Afghanistan War, which was also based on lies, because if you look at what really happened on Sept. 11, then Article Five of NATO should not have been invoked. Then you had the murder of Qaddafi. Look at what all of these countries now look like. Then you had the attempt to overthrow Assad. You can add Yemen. You can add Palestine. So, the whole region from Afghanistan to the North of Africa is a nightmare.

And, as a result of it, because of various dubious policies, to say the least, of the Obama Administration in support, first of the mujahideen, then al-Qaeda, then Al Nusra, then ISIS, you have now a situation where the largest refugee crisis since the Second World War has erupted. There are now every day, tens of thousands of people coming from mainly Syria, but also Iraq, Afghanistan, and other war-torn regions, and this is clearly over-stretching the capacity of Europe. People arrive, this direction, and I can only stay in power if I go with the majority; being a truthful politician, so she took the initiative.

I think other factors were involved, because in the recent period, there were many, many people in Europe who warned that we are on the edge of World War III. Helmut Schmidt, who is 95 years old, and Gorbachov, who's not liked in Russia but the Germans always liked "Gorby," warned three times in a row that we are at the verge of World War III. The head of the Duma, Naryshkin, said if it comes to World War III, this will be the last one of mankind because nobody will survive it.

Bundesregierung/Kugler

German Chancellor Angela Merkel addresses members of various refugee groups in Berlin Sept. 10, on Germany's open-door policy to the massive influx.

You had the European Leadership Network, which is a thinktank of former defense ministers and military analysts, who put out three papers within six weeks, saying we are heading towards war, towards nuclear war. The first paper said "NATO is preparing a war against Russia and Russia is preparing a war against NATO," and therefore we have to have urgently new rules of dialogue, of communication, which does not exist any more, urging that such a code of behavior must be urgently established.

So, while the normal person on the street may not know all the reasons, the geopolitics behind it, the fact that the trans-Atlantic financial system is about to blow out in a much bigger way than 2008, yet people in the last weeks have changed in all of Europe. We have information tables in many countries, and therefore we have a good reading on what is the mood in the population; and I think it was the combination of the euro crisis,—people knew that if Greece would go in an unorderly exit, you could have an instant blowout of the entire financial system.

So people were caught in between anxiety because of world war, worry about the economic security because of the euro collapsing, and naturally then the refugee crisis on top of it. I think it dawned on people, all of a sudden, and this soap bubble, which people were in the whole time, popped; and people realized, "Hey, wait a second. This civilization is about to crash against the wall and we have to change." That, I think, led to a situation where people opened their hearts, and responded

to the refugee crisis. I think the last time you had an expression of popular will like that, was when the Wall came down, and with the peaceful revolution, the peaceful demonstrations, the Monday demonstrations, in what became then east Germany, and what was the G.D.R. before, which brought down the Wall. And the present mood in the population is approaching exactly that quality.

Now with that goes something else and that is what I referred to as the *Erinyes*, the idea, in this beautiful poem by Friedrich Schiller, the *Cranes of Ibykus*, which you should all read when you get home—we have a book where this is published also and translated,—that there is a higher power, that you can't commit crimes for a very long time; that God is not an old man with a beard Who immediately, if somebody robs their neighbor, comes down with the lightning and strikes people down. It's not like that at all.

But there is something which is called natural law. The Chinese call it the Mandate of Heaven, and in all great cultures you have this idea that there is a higher lawfulness which man cannot defy forever. And I think we are, at this point, experiencing such a moment where a great crime is awakening many, many peoples around the world, and it is a moment of change, and we must absolutely not miss that moment.

Because what went along with the refugee crisis is suddenly people saying, wait a second; where do these refugees come from? It is the United States. It is the wars which were conducted by the United States in the Middle East, and it is the support of terrorist organizations, to eliminate and replace legitimate sovereign governments. Now, you don't have to be a friend of Saddam Hussein, of Assad, of Qaddafi, but the reality is when these people, who may have been dictators or not,—I mean, democracy is not such a thing to cherish so much, because where is democracy in the United States? Where is democracy in Europe? [applause] So these people have been called dictators, and you don't have to like them. I have no particular sympathy for any of them.

But if you look at how they were running their countries—Iraq, with Saddam Hussein, had a functioning infrastructure, a functioning university system; women could study. You look at Libya, Qaddafi was involved in infrastructure development not only in Libya but in Africa. It was a functioning country. Syria before this happened, was a country where you had a very functioning collaboration of all religions who peacefully lived together, Christians, Muslims of different types, other people, and now?

Look at what has happened now! You have Wahhabi Salafists trying to destroy the memory of humanity about its cultural goods. The bombing of the Baghdad museum—there was no military reason for it. U.S. General Schwarzkopf, who promised to bomb Iraq back into the Dark Age, did a pretty good job fulfilling his promise. Then you look at what happened recently with the ancient city of Palmyra. It was flattened. In Afghanistan, the large Buddhist sculptures. These people are trying to eradicate the memory of culture, which is universal history.

So, don't tell me there was anything good coming out of these wars. You have a situation where even some former American diplomats are making public speeches, to say that even from a narrow American interest, this is a failed policy from Cheney, Bush, to Obama without interruption, because the same neo-con apparatus is running both administrations. Even from a narrow American standpoint, if the objective is to increase American influence in the region: complete failure. So why is there not a movement in the United States that says: Yes, these are failed policies and we need to correct them.

The Promise of the BRICS

Now, on the optimist side, I was very happy that the Senator was praising China so much, because it is a different model of working together of nations. Not only has China developed the idea of Confucian economics. It's a meritocracy. It's maybe still a little communist, but I think that can really be neglected, because the Confucian element is so much stronger in what the present Chinese government does: the emphasis on education, the emphasis on brilliance, on excellence of young people, of bringing the best minds forward, of having as many people as possible participating in the best possible education. And offering a model of collaboration based on win-win, on sovereignty, on respect for the other social system. And they have offered to the United States a collaboration on equal footing. So why not take that offer?

The BRICS countries have developed a completely alternative model of economics, of great projects, of overcoming underdevelopment, and it's steadily progressing. Just now, China had a big conference with leaders from the Arab world. Now, when I read that, I was extremely happy because, how are the hell are we going to bring peace to the Middle East? Obviously, and from everything we know, President Putin will make a speech at the United Nations General Assembly, where he will demand and offer an international coalition to fight terrorism, and other forms of extremism.

I know that Germany, for example, is already backing a flanking move, which Russia just did in Syria by moving its military there, because they don't want to have the last secular government in the region wiped out. Now, the United States government was completely caught by surprise. They said, "why didn't we see this coming?" The CIA said, "Oh, we missed that one..." But, what is the NSA good for, if they're spying on everybody, when they can't even catch a move like that?

Now you have a situation where Germany has already backed the Russian move in Syria. Hollande is backing it. Even the British are forced to realign their view on it. So, when Putin makes a speech in the United Nations, saying we need to have an international coalition against terrorism, if the United States should turn out to be the only country opposing it, that would really make them look very bad. So I hope that they use the remaining days to think through this question very well, and make up their mind to join this coalition.

Because what we need to do, is not only to end this terrorism, but we have to eliminate the root of terrorism, and that is *poverty*. The only way that we will bring back peace to the Middle East, is by taking the BRICS conception of a "win-win" collaboration of all the participating countries, of extending the New Silk Road—the idea of rebuilding the ancient Silk Road with modern means, modern technology, modern infrastructure, and extend it to become the "World Land-Bridge."

We—*EIR*, the Schiller Institute—have produced a 370-page study, with the title "The New Silk Road Becomes the World Land-Bridge," which is the idea of taking that conception, in a certain sense take an economic miracle, like the United States did it repeatedly, with Lincoln, with Franklin D. Roosevelt, with Kennedy; or Germany did it after the Second World War, with the German Economic Miracle; or China has been doing it for the last 30 years, where China developed in 30 years what other major nations needed 200 years for!

And China is now offering that Chinese economic miracle as a model of economic development for all the countries who want to be part of it. And it is moving quite nicely: Latin America is already part of it; large parts of Asia are part of it; Africa is very much interested in it. The Egyptian President el-Sisi, has just completed the second Suez Canal, in *one year*. And, that is part of the Chinese Maritime Silk Road.

So, when I read that the Chinese just conducted a conference with the Arab leaders, and they responded very well to the idea of having economic development in the Middle East, I was extremely happy. Because this is what we proposed in 2012, where we said we have to

have a solution where Russia, China, India, Iran, Egypt, and hopefully Germany, Italy, France, the United States, all work together to develop the Middle East economically. We have to give a perspective especially to young people, that they want to study, in order to be able to raise a family, rather than joining the jihadis; where we have to offer them something where they start to love you, instead of hating you. I mean, the only way that we will ever come out of this is, stop the hate! Stop this destruction! Stop the drones! For every drone killing a terrorist, you are creating 50 new terrorists! Have we not learned that lesson?

So, we have to replace this policy of destruction, of militarization, which doesn't serve anybody except a couple of billionaires.

And look, the United States is falling apart! Have you travelled recently over a highway? Have you tried to go by car from Washington to New York? Your chance of ending up in a pothole, is higher than winning the Nobel Prize! [laughter] Well, that's not a good proportion. But anyway, if you go by the train, how many miles of the fast train system has the United States built in the last decades? *None*. Zero. How many has China built? I think it's around 18,000 km right now. The goal

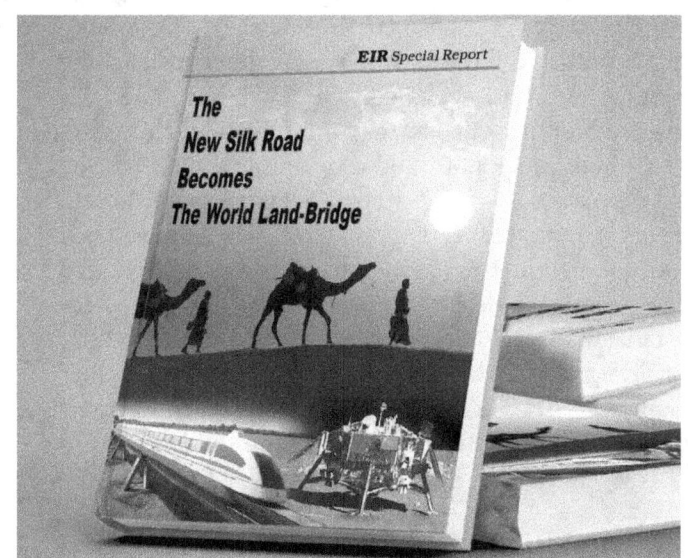

is 50,000 by 2020-something. But, they have already built 18,000! I was lucky enough to travel from Beijing to Shanghai with one of these Chinese-engineered made fast trains, and it goes 310 km; and you can take your water, fill it to the brim and not one drop falls out of it, because they go smooth, quick, quiet—more quiet than this room! [laughter]

Gravel: Siemens. Siemens is the one that built that technology. Isn't that maglev?

Zepp-LaRouche: Well, no, no. The train I went on was a Chinese-engineered technology. I'm not talking about the maglev, no. This was a different fast-train system.

CC/Khalidshou

China has now developed its own high-speed train. Here a CRH380A model leaves Shanghai's Hongqiao Station in 2010.

I'm saying, why can we not create a movement in the United States, which says: If the United States joins the Silk Road, joins the World Land-Bridge, rather than wasting all this investment in military products—which is not so great anymore, anyway; you know the Chinese are just outdoing you there too?

And why can we not build an infrastructure in the United States, have fast train systems connecting the East Coast; replace obsolete, old airplanes by having maglev trains, or other fast trains? And reconstruct the United States! Build a couple of new cities! The Chinese are building one new city after the other; why can the United States not build a dozen new cities in the middle part, east of the Rocky Mountains? This is a pretty depopulated, underpopulated area. And we need to do something, in any case, in order to fight the drought and the desert. So, when we go to new water systems, like ionization of water over the ocean to fight the drought in Texas and in California, and the other Southern states, let's just build a couple of cities! New science cities, beautiful cities! I'm for building a beautiful city in the United States! [applause]

A Mass Movement for Development

So, I think that what we need to do, is really have a Renaissance movement. Narendra Modi, the Prime Minister of India, called for a mass movement for development, and I think that's what we need in the United States. Because, you have to get the sense that there is a chance to turn the situation around.

China is progressing, offering a "win-win" cooperation. Germany, they are already increasing the number of people who say, "Wait a second, for us to work with the Silk Road would be so much more profitable, than being drawn into wars against Russia with sanctions, which is hurting us more than even Russia." Russia can go to China, to India—they're reorienting! But, Germany is about to lose—Germany exports machine tools, machine tool design, and some of these take five years to build! These are not things you just "pop out" like popcorn; these are things which need planning, designing, tooling for specific purposes; and when sanctions ruined that, and you lose a market, you lose it forever. And that is the fear in the German industry right now, if the sanctions are maintained, then extremely important relations between Germany and Russia will be lost, for economic purposes.

People are thinking the same thing in France, in Italy. So, there is right now a groundswell to stop the sanctions. But obviously the question is, will people have the courage to buck the United States? Because that is really the bottom line of all of this.

What I'm really doing is, I'm calling upon you to become even more active than you are already. We have the United Nations General Assembly, and I wrote an appeal to this effect, and in my view, maybe, and Lyn said the same thing, it may really be the last chance for humanity to change course. You have an extraordinary number of political leaders—Xi Jinping will come, Putin will come, the Pope will come, other important people will come; and we should create an atmosphere in New York, and around the United States to say: "Enough is enough! We want the United States to join with these other countries to build the world, and stop wars based on lies and support of terrorists, one organization after the other!"

I think if we get enough motion by people who say, it is really time for the United States to be a republic again, and not try to be an empire, and have a unipolar world, based on the Project for a New American Century doctrine, which is really what is working here still; that the United States will not allow any country or a number of countries, to come up and be superior or even equal—that policy has to stop! The United States must accept they are not the only superpower anymore.

Nobody wants to deny the United States a role. They should have a role. They should be part of the nations as John Quincy Adams said. I don't mind if the United States wants to be the *primus inter pares*, the first among equals; that's fine! But you are not the only one,

and that is what has to be said very clearly as a message.

So, I think it's really a moment, where everything depends on the subjective factor. Because objectively, all the elements for change are there. And you have to be aware that many times, you cannot change anything, because structures are cemented; it looks as if you can't really do much because you have alliances, you have processes, treaties, and nothing moves forward. But, then come, from time to time, what I call the "star hours of history" [*Sternstunden der Menschheit*]: '89 was such a moment, when the Wall came down, and the German reunification was the result of it: that was a "star hour of history."

I know that we are now in this kind of a period. We may not be at a November '89, but I think we are like October '89. You can see it coming, and it comes like a groundswell, where both the forces of destruction are accelerating, but also the forces of construction and of the Good are also moving.

Everything will depend on the Americans. Because if America joins this world movement for development, everything can be solved.

So please, live up to the moment of history! [applause]

It is Feasible to Dump Obama and End This Plan of War

Speed: Now we're going right to our question and answer period.

Q: Hello, I'm E— from Russian Center, New York, and I thank you very much, Helga, for such a nice presentation. I have one question which bothers me a lot, and I'm very concerned. Recently, you talked about this move—Russian military to Syria. Is there any chance that Americans would back a Russian initiative? Or do you think it's going to be the opposite? I'm a little bit concerned about this confrontation between U.S. troops and Russian troops, so what do you think is the possibility that they can really come together and fight ISIS at this point?

Zepp-LaRouche: I think it's not totally decided yet. And I'm not saying I have the last information on it; I'm only going on press reports, which say that the White House was completely caught by surprise. And that there is a big faction fight where one faction says, why don't we just work with the Russians and stabilize Assad, because ISIS is the bigger problem? And there is another faction which is against that. So I don't think it's yet decided.

But I think it was a true flank. You know, when you are confronted with an almost unsolvable problem, an excellent military commander always thinks about the flank; you don't bang your head against the wall in a head-to-head confrontation. Obviously, the situation in Syria had reached a point where, because Erdogan had bombed the PKK, and the PKK was practically the most efficient force outside the Syrian army to fight ISIS; and Erdogan had about two years ago requested Patriot missiles from the United States, Holland and Germany, and they were moved there and they had created a no-fly zone over parts of Syria, since the range of these Patriot missiles was much larger than to the Turkish border.

That no-fly zone allowed ISIS to advance almost to

UN/Joshua Kristal

President Vladimir Putin at his last appearance at the UN General Assembly, in September 2005. His intervention this year, scheduled for September 28, holds the potential for revolutionary change internationally.

the suburbs of Damascus. And at that point, either Russia would have done nothing, and then the danger would have been that ISIS takes over Damascus; and, as you know, Russia has this naval port Tartous, and it's building a second naval military facility a little bit further north.

At that point the question was, and people realized that if ISIS takes over all of Syria, then the next countries falling would be Jordan and Lebanon. And it is estimated that if that happened, then terrorism would, in a limitless way, go after Europe everywhere. And naturally it is a security threat also for Russia, because a lot of the ISIS fighters are Chechens; for China, because they are into Xinjiang, and working with the Uighurs. So there is a European, Chinese, Russian interest to stop this, because you know this is a barbaric phenomenon.

Obama Thrown Off-Balance

So Putin then made this surprise move. Probably it was planned for a long time, to coincide also with the United Nations General Assembly. And I think that it really makes it so obvious where is right and where is wrong at this point, and I just hope there are enough military, diplomats, intelligence people, in the United States who say that the best way to get out of this is that the United States would join hands with Russia to do this. And that the moment will be at the United Nations General Assembly. In the time between now and then, we must all activate, multiply our own efforts to cause the international community to demand that. Because where should be the place to discuss that, if not in the United Nations General Assembly? That is the only available world court, so to speak; the whole world is looking at it; that's the place where you can bring it up.

So let's make a gigantic effort that this becomes the change which is so urgently needed.

Speed: Lyn, let me just ask you, do you have any response to that?

LaRouche: No, I think Helga does a good job when she wants to do it. [Laughter.]

Q: Good afternoon, this is J— W—, from Brooklyn, New York, and I want to first address Mr. La-Rouche. Good afternoon, Mr. LaRouche, how are you doing? And I want to say that I'm sorry I missed your birthday party. I had to take care of my grandson, who is really cute, by the way, and I will be at the next one, okay?

And with that said, this is my question. It's something in the same vein of the young woman who just spoke. We have seen President Obama, a puppet of the British Empire, promise to fight terrorism while introducing economic and military policies that actually escalate terrorism. Now last week, Mr. LaRouche enlightened us as to the history of the destruction of the cooperation between Israel and other nations in the region, by the British and British-run operations. And we know that in somewhat the same way, British operations have been enhanced in the U.S. through despicable policies put in place under the noses of the Ameri-

can people.

Now, in the same vein, the Israel government, and I want to make it clear that I am not talking against the Jewish people of Israel, or any other Jewish groups; I'm talking about the government of Israel and their policies that support the Al Nusra, which is an ally of al-Qaeda and ISIS in Syria. With the United Nations meeting next week, right here in New York City, by the way, what do you feel,—and this is for Helga, or for Mr. La-Rouche,—what do you feel Putin will have to do to deal with Israel, and at the same time, garner support from other nations, in his plan to deal with ISIS, and therefore, indirectly, deal with Obama?

LaRouche: I would say, in this case, that what Putin has done has actually thrown Obama off balance, and things have to be taken from that standpoint of reference. I've followed this thing carefully, and I've watched what Putin was doing, and I began to warn some of our people what was up, what was really happening. That Putin acted to exploit the stupidity of Obama, and Obama brought defeat upon himself.

Now, we hope that defeat is more than permanent, to get rid of him. We want him out of the government under the 25th Amendment, which provides for such actions. But what the issue is, is that there is actually a peace movement implicit in what Putin did. It's not simply some accident, some coincidence.

If you look carefully, you look what happened in the course of this thing in terms of Germany. Now Germany was in a totally accepted submission to Obama on this question of policy. That disappeared. It disappeared when Germany supported the poor refugees, who were facing death in parts of Europe, especially in Germany. You find other developments like that; that Obama's destiny is downward. It could be permanently downward. We would hope that the result of the discussions during the coming meetings of this month, will actually bring the Obama Ddministration out of existence. That Obama will go someplace else, let him not do this any more. Let's get rid of other people. Huh? Cheney, Dick Cheney, "Dirty Dick" Cheney, another one of these characters. And if Bush had any brains, he'd be dangerous.

Therefore the problem is of that nature, that we have a situation where Putin has acted, opportunely, to deal with the opportunity which was presented by the foolishness of Obama. In other words, Obama's own greed and stupidity have been the instrument by which his future is being destroyed now.

White House/Pete Souza

Neither Israeli Prime Minister Benjamin Netanyahu (left) nor Barack Obama, both de facto British agents, can look forward to a promising future. Here they prepare to talk in the Oval Office on March 5, 2012.

drive Netanyahu from office at some point in the next year or so.

And maybe I'm just wishful thinking and hoping that's the case, but you've got to keep in mind that the Jewish community is not of one voice any more. It was for a great deal of time. What's unfortunate is that the Jewish community, the wealthy people, are older and conservative. And so therefore those are the ones that have been pushing the policies that have been foisted on the United States Congress. And bear in mind, that now that the Republicans have taken over in their association with the Jewish Community to the detriment, political detriment, of Democrats, that in itself is an earth-shaking development.

Speed: Senator Gravel wants to...

Gravel: I'd like to add a little comment on something that's barely been touched on. If you look very closely, you realize that the United States foreign policy in the Middle East has been dictated out of Tel Aviv and Jerusalem. [Applause] And it operates through AIPAC primarily, and I've had my run-ins with AIPAC then and since.

But I think you must appreciate that this [the failure of the Congress to kill the P5+1 deal-ed.] is the first time, no the second time, in my knowledge, that AIPAC lost out, or the Jewish community leadership lost out in a confrontation over an issue. The last time was when I voted with respect to others on the jets to Sadat, which were opposed by AIPAC. And I've seen instances where a White House decision was made at 9 o'clock, and by 10:30 there was a majority letter, signed by a majority number of Senators opposing that policy. It worked like magic. But this is the first time that you've seen the Democratic Senators [do this], other than the three who have gone along with Netanyahu.

Now we've really got to thank Netanyahu for what he's done for us. Because what he's done, in my mind, is break the back of the power of what the Israeli government has over the United States. You're going to see this played out. There's going to be payback in the political process with respect with Netanyahu. And I would suspect that this defeat they've suffered will

Planet Ponzi

And so what is going to happen as a result of this? Either it will neutralize any influence that we have, and we have very little in the Middle East with respect to being an honest broker, because we're not, never have been, and I don't think we can ever become an honest broker. No. Will Putin and others move into this category? I think we are going to see this at the UN General Assembly.

I'll be speaking at the press club, which is the association of reporters at the UN, at 11 o'clock on Monday, and I'll be carrying the same message about the importance of the Chinese moves, of the loss of influence of the Jewish community on the American body politic, and where the future lies. And I must say, I know you are very enamored of the fact that the United States should and could; and the problem is that it hasn't in the past, and if it doesn't, the question is who is going to do it? And I think it will be a combination of China and Russia, and what I think we can hope for with the influence of your organization, is to get us to go along with that leadership. That's my hope on it.

But bear in mind that this was a very cataclysmic change in power that was suffered by the leadership of the Jewish community in the United States of America.

Q: Hi there Senator, Helga, Mr. LaRouche. My name is Mitch Feierstein. I'm an investment banker and the author of a book called *Planet Ponzi*, which discusses the debt and the debt problem that we have. I believe that the situation that we have is not sustainable—the $230 trillion that the U.S. has in debt. There were several good points that were made here today about the European Union and about the BRICS. For people who don't know who the BRICS are, it's Brazil, Russia, India, and China.

Gravel: And South Africa.

Q: [follow-up] Sorry, and South Africa.

So I think that what we need to talk about is how we got into the state that we're in. There's too much debt, too much credit, and too much leverage, which started when Glass-Steagall [was repealed] under Larry Summers, the Treasury Secretary, and Robert Rubin who's ex-Goldman Sachs came in. What's happened is the debt has escalated from 1999 to the beginning of the credit crisis in 2007. China's debt has gone up from $6 trillion in the past six years to over $30 trillion. Russia, on the other hand, is probably the only country that runs a surplus.

An International Opening

What we're seeing now is the European Union is falling apart, with the mass of immigration from Syria and the countries where our foreign policy has failed. So I guess my question to you would be, if you could go back 25 years ago and look at what our economic policy has been, and the foundations by Larry Summers and Paul Krugman and the same people, does it strike you that Albert Einstein summed it up best when he said, "Insanity is doing the same thing over and over and expecting to achieve a different result?"

LaRouche: I would reply to that proposition on two points. First of all, Einstein is the proper person to refer to, if you understand the entire history of the U.S. economy since the beginning of the Twentieth Century, because we have been in a long period of moral decline, despite things like Franklin Roosevelt. And Kennedy was a great President, actually, if he hadn't been killed, and his brother hadn't been killed.

Ryan Lawler

One of the biggest sources of inflation in the U.S. economy—the New York Stock Exchange.

The problem lies in the idea of Wall Street. Wall Street is the center of this, because what's the situation now? Wall Street is hopelessly *bankrupt*. It's *super-bankrupt*. What keeps Wall Street alive is an inflation, in worthless Wall Street money, and as long as people believe that that money which passes through Wall Street and pays off a few people, as long as they trust that, they're going to be suckers. And Einstein, of course, is the kind of person who would cause a problem about that.

But what we're faced with now, we have to do very simply. There's a very simple solution here. We have to simply go back to a Glass-Steagall policy, the one of President Franklin Roosevelt, exactly. Now, Franklin Roosevelt's policy in this regard is somewhat outdated, because the conditions have been outdated, but in principle, if you apply the principle rather than the details, his policy was the policy which is now required. Because all of Wall Street, *the whole shebang*, is absolutely worthless and should be closed down immediately!

Now, with this thing that's happening this month now, we have an opening, an international opening, because around the world similar kinds of conditions exist. France is in a mess, Italy is almost destroyed, Spain is almost destroyed, Portugal—you can't even find it, that's how bad it is. So these and related kinds of things all come together with the problem in the United States. This is the time for an international Glass-Steagall reform, which cleans up the mess, and waste and fraud, which is shared among various nations. And by cutting out this artificial inflation,—and it is artificial inflation,—when an agency under the power of government begins creating investments which are non-value, that is no value, and no value whatsoever to mankind,—that system has to come to an end on a global scale.

Now this reference to Russia's policy in this question is relevant, but it's not the solution. It can be part of the solution, but what we need to do is actually,—and the United States should do it,—throw Obama out of office right now. We have the 25th Amendment to do that job. Immediately go into a Glass-Steagall reform, which means you cancel Wall Street, all those values which are called Wall Street values, which are fake values, *cancel them*.

We can take the properties in Manhattan, for example, which have this kind of occupation and say, "What's your income worth," and they don't have much to say. So some agency, of course, like a Franklin Roosevelt agency, would have to step in and organize a redemption of those properties which have some functional use, and use that as one of the ways of getting the reconstruction of the U.S. economy. And doing that will mean that the United States will be highly devoted to what that will have created, and I think that other nations will be equally affected.

Q: [follow-up] I think that one thing I'll follow with is T-TIP, you know the trade agreement that is a secret agreement. The United States has gone from a republic to a republic-democracy, and from democracy to plutocracy, and we're headed towards tyranny, where we're not even allowed to see what this agreement is all about. The Federal Reserve, which is a bunch of non-elected officials under Janet Yellen, and Ben Bernanke, and predecessor Greenspan, have run their balance sheet up to over $5 trillion. And as you rightly pointed out, Mr. LaRouche, the guarantees that were given to Wall Street were over $100 trillion. So our country is not in a position right now where we can get out from underneath the debt, so U.S. dollar hegemony is going to come to a rapid end, I think sooner than a lot of people think. Thanks for your thoughts on that. What do you think about the dollar?

The Israeli Case

LaRouche: [laughs] I think we can recreate the dollar.

Gravel: Today,—and it's very historic,—the person who has taken over the leadership of the Labour Party, which is the only alternative government that exists to Cameron, is a person, essentially his views are the same as Bernie Sanders. And one of the major platform issues is he wants to institute the concept of Glass-Steagall in Britain, if he's elected to take over the government. So this is a significant occurrence today. I don't know if you're aware of it. This could be as earthshaking as what I think happened to Netanyahu.

Q: Good afternoon. Mr. Lyndon, Helga. I was born in Russia, I came to the United States 20 years ago, the most beautiful country in the world. If I, being a Russian, go to Germany, for example, I would still be a Russian in Germany. But the only country in the world in which I can become a citizen is the United States. I love the United States, but I'm very surprised by the people who control the United States for the simple reason that they're not even Americans. The people who control the United States—these are not Americans. So my feedback on Syria is, see after Sept. 11, Afghanistan, Iraq, Syria, Libya; so my feedback on that, it's got nothing to do with Sept. 11. I studied history when I was younger, and I realized that history always repeats itself. So, Roman mentality was "divide and conquer." Once you make a chaos, it's easy to control. And once something happens, you should see who benefits the most.

So I think the crisis which is happening in the Middle East right now, if you think who would benefit from the turmoil. My mom was a Jew, so basically, I'm half-Russian, half-Jewish, so it could be your truth, it could be my truth, it could be whole truth, it's in general.

So the Jews for 2,000 years, they want to rebuild Solomon's Temple, because if you don't make a sacrifice in the Temple you're not redeemed. The people who control this country are the Masons—you can check this out—they truly believe the Temple should be rebuilt. So that's what they believe in. So basically, my point of view right now is, they want to make all this chaos; you see, where the Solomon Temple is right now in Israel, there are two holy Muslim spots, which cannot be removed. But once the Middle East becomes turmoil, you can do anything you want to do.

So basically, I'm thinking, that's one of the biggest reasons why the situation in the Middle East is the way it is: The Masons want to rebuild the Temple for one reason; the Jews want to rebuild the Temple for another reason. But it all comes down to the same thing.

Me, personally, I truly believe there is a God, who engineered it all. Once I came to this country 20 years ago, I see all the spots, "God Bless America, God Bless America." I don't see it any more, I'll be honest with you. If I was to say to somebody "God bless you," he would look at me like I'm crazy. I've been honest with you, but I truly believe in that God engineered it for a reason, for a purpose, or we come from monkeys, so make a decision. I truly believe I came from God. I'm finished.

LaRouche: I can answer this thing. I think the point is, I think it's the wrong emphasis, because the point is, we think on details. We think on a detailed experience, a local one. That doesn't make any sense to me.

I look at a longer term, say the period of the Great Renaissance, the Great Renaissance in Europe, for example. And that was destroyed. That was destroyed by a later development. And then there was a development again. Leibniz, for example, was one of the people like Kepler before him, who created a whole civilization. The civilization was essentially international. It does not mean that it included directly all nations, but the process of civilization has been international, in the main.

If you want to account for these things, you try to pick some particular deal, and you say, wait a minute; let's stop right there. Isn't this a part of a larger operation, which is doing it?

Now, the case of the Israeli case, I'm quite familiar with it, because I was involved in this when the Israeli organization was being created, as a military organization. And I associated myself with that institution, and as long as it lived, it was a so-called socialistic union. And they were a military operation. And I was in close support of them, for my own capacity, and I had people who were going into Israel, Jewish persons who going into Israel, to colonize the area.

And then they got knocked out, by whom? By the British Empire! And a British Empire election did it. And then you had assassinations of leading figures, Jewish figures in Israel, who were knocked out again and again by the British control,—and what you have in Israel right now is, you have the British system is controlling Israel right now from the top down. We should hope that that will be changed, very soon.

The Sources of Corruption

Q: Good afternoon. My name is M— G—, and I've been a student of history my whole life, and I thoroughly enjoyed it up to a few years ago, when I realized most of what I learned was all lies. [laughter] And so, it's now a re-investigation of all history that makes it interesting. What I've also learned is that we really don't have a government in the United States. What we have is basically treasonous paid-for prostitutes.

So, with that being said, there seem to be secret organizations that Kennedy spoke of, such as the Trilateral Commission, the Bilderberg Group, the Illuminati, Council on Foreign Affairs; and I believe within those groups, there's between three and five hundred men that control the whole planet. And the true Axis of Evil is the U.S. government, the British government, and the Israeli government, because they're the ones creating all the hostilities in the world, and that are perpetuating the wars.

My question to you gentlemen,—which I have to tell you, I'm astounded the amount of wisdom and honesty that I had to come to a Manhattan basement to learn, after listening to my government for 54 years,— not including Kennedy, of course, because I loved him. But the rest of the B.S. I've heard my whole life just makes me want to vomit. And I think there's more intelligence here than the whole group of people running for President, or that we've had.

So hopefully one of you gentlemen, or this young lady here, runs for President, because you're certainly smarter than all the people running for President put together right now.

LaRouche: I don't know if Helga wants to get involved in that!

Q: [follow-up] So, basically, I personally feel that these secret organizations are at their zenith of power,— and they are the ones controlling it. And you know, we talk of Obama. The guy's a puppet, just like the rest of the government, and to me they're just evil people, but they're being controlled. In your opinions, who's really pulling the strings? Who are really the bad guys?

LaRouche: Well, the history is, the British Empire is still today the one answer. Most corruption in the United States came from the Southerners. Why? Because the Southern part of the United States was corrupt from its conception, in opposition to our greatest leaders at that time. And repeatedly, we've had repeated things. Who were behind this? The *British Empire was behind it*, all of it.

Q: [Follow-up] I suspect we're kind of vague in that, and maybe if people are a little reluctant to throw names out, I will, and tell me if I'm right. The Rothschilds, Soros, Rockefeller—are they the bad guys?

LaRouche: They're part of it, but that's only a small part. You have many people in government in the United States, who fit the same category. You see it on

---

Now, our Constitutional system, when properly advised, will lead in the direction of the answer. Because, what's the answer? The answer is, that each generation of mankind, all people are going to die. All human beings are going to die. We know of no case where there's an exception. So, what's the answer? Will the next generation of people be able to make a contribution to the future of mankind, and mankind's behavior?

---

the street. You see it in people who don't even know that they are evil, and doing evil things. They have evil ideas; their religious beliefs, or similar things. No, the corruption is *not* the individuals. The corruption lies in the process. That's been the history. And our history of the United States, particularly with Alexander Hamilton's study, and what he did, as opposed to what his opponents did. And that's the real story.

The idea that there are particular bad people running loose. Yeah, I know about the mafia. They're bad people. I know that. But the mafia is *not* the instrument of evil. It is merely the errand boys of local evil. So, the issues have to go deeper. They go to matters of principle, not to gossip.

What is Money?

Gravel: There was a study done years back in Switzerland by an institute, and what they studied was the aggregation of wealth in the hands of institutions, and they looked at 45,000 institutions that were of a transnational nature. And they winnowed it down to 1500 institutions who controlled the majority, substantial majority, of the world's wealth. These institutions were basically—the top ten were banks, and the others were the families that you associate... And so, when you talk about the Bilderberg, and the Trilateral, these are people who get together for their enlightened self-interest, as

they perceive it. And they make various deals in that regard.

Q: [follow-up] ...geopolitics, and decide who and what it's going to be...

Gravel: Yeah, in a *de facto* kind of way. But as Lyndon was just saying, it's a little deeper than that. It has a moral component to it, that if you're a billionaire, you don't understand the rest of the people, just don't understand, and it's not within their moral comprehension about equality. Because what you think is that this is a God-given right, or gift, that you've got, because you're a billionaire. And so, that's the group of people who essentially operate the economic systems.

What I really liked, Lyndon, was when Lagarde, who heads up the IMF, said that the solution to Greece was just, forget their debt. And I would like to see a concept—and you may want to comment on this—a concept that we use the bankruptcy principle. And that is, that the world's bankrupt, the U.S. is bankrupt, but let's just wipe out all this debt! Who gets hurt with that? The bankers. And they'll write this off, and the world will start a new economic beginning, and burgeoning. So, that's my take on what you said.

Q: Speaking of China getting stronger in the world through development, this past week, ground was broken, I believe, in Springfield, Massachusetts for a company to start building trains, and the company—I forget the name, but it was a company from China—Oh, my name is G—from Massachusetts, and my question is: How do we replace the likes of Boehner, McConnell, as well as Obama, and move to working with the BRICS nations?

LaRouche: Well, what you're asking is a broad question, which is often mentioned, but without a solution being attached to the question. The thing is, this is not really where it's located. Look, it's located in questions of policy. And the question is not the individual *per se*. It's a question of policy.

What do you mean by policy? You mean the Constitution. Well, if you pick up the Constitution, how is it observed? Is it being actually observed? Or was there an error in it? And these are the things that will decide what will be done efficiently. What will be done as a matter of apparent comment, is not relevant. Because people just don't have that kind of knowledge. They all have ideas about what is wrong, what is right, but they don't know what they're talking about.

For example, take the case of money. And most of this stuff calls to money. Now, what is money, and how is money understood? Well, that's nonsense. Money has no intrinsic value. *Money has no intrinsic value.* And so all the stuff about speculation on money doesn't solve the question, the essential question. Because, for example, we're talking about mankind.

Anthony Berger/Brady National Photographics Art Gallery

President Abraham Lincoln with his son Tad.

We're not talking about animals. We're talking about mankind. And what defines mankind's appropriate behavior as mankind? And that's what you apply. You don't try to find out who's wrong, who's doing this, who's doing that. Everybody can be wrong. The question is, are you going to solve the problem? Are you going to identify...?

What's the problem? Well, are you going to produce a child, whom you develop, who is going to be a better scientist than you are? And that's the standard. We have a system of money, and a system of policy, which is based on the wrong values.

Now, our Constitutional system, when properly advised, will lead in the direction of the answer. Because what's the answer? The answer is, that each generation of mankind, all people are going to die. All human beings are going to die. We know of no case where there's an exception. So, what's the answer? Will the next generation of people be able to make a contribution to the future of mankind, and mankind's behavior?

The green policy, for example,—anybody who supports the green policy, is an

> Because the requirement for mankind is that mankind must develop the human species to a higher level. That is, to a higher level. There's really an authentic religious meaning to it. That mankind is the only species which has this gift of immorality, in that nature. And it's the maintenance of that behavior, and the behavior that goes with that, which realizes the intention of a Creator.

enemy of mankind, in principle. Because the requirement for mankind is that mankind must develop the human species to a higher level. That is, to a higher level. There's really an authentic religious meaning to it. That mankind is the only species which has this gift of immortality in that nature. And it's the maintenance of that behavior, and the behavior that goes with that, which realizes the intention of a Creator.

That's the basis on which all morality has to be based. Otherwise it's just junk. It's gossip.

Obama and Iran

Q: Hi, Mr. LaRouche. I am K— from the Bronx. When we are told a lie, and we believe the lie, and then we are told the truth, we go on believing the lie. I am having a very great deal of difficulty wrapping my brain around Obama trying to do something, anything, beneficial to this country or to the world. My concern is the Iranian agreement. I don't approve of sanctions; I don't feel they benefit. I realize Iran has a right to their money. I am very concerned about how they're going to use their money. I'm afraid they're going to create a lot of harm with it.

Now, Obama is leading us into thermonuclear war, and yet we are being told—I think it's coming from LaRouche—that the Iranian agreement is going to lead to peace. How can Obama take us into a thermonuclear war, and create peace on the other hand?

I understand that Russia is moving, and I do believe they are moving as best they can towards trying to create a peaceful world, and I see that a new paradigm is being created, and Iran is an ally of Russia. Is Russia going to draw Iran into a more peaceful mentality? That's really my question.

LaRouche: The answer essentially is Obama. Obama is the immediate factor, most relevant immediate factor in that problem right now. I know I've dealt with this thing with Iran, and I understand it. It's gone through various stages of evolution, since the time of the overthrow of the old Shah. You're absolutely right on this thing. This is simply a matter of understanding a higher value, that the standard is, what does mankind require? And what is mankind that mankind should require a solution of that type? And we try to get people to come to an agreement, and not do harm to one another. And I think if you have the right kind of environment, and can maintain it, you can carry out that policy.

Gravel: I want to speak directly to that. I've been to Tehran. I've keynoted a conference over there. I'm interviewed almost weekly by PressTV, and I've got to tell you, you've got nothing to worry about from Iran. Nothing at all, nothing at all. And what they're going to use that money for: They'll use it for themselves, and they'll use it for their allies. Who are their allies? Hezbollah. Here, the American government has defined Hezbollah as a terrorist organization. That's because of Israel's view on that.

So, we support Israel, and they do some terrible things. Are we a terrorist country because of that? The Non-Proliferation Treaty is very clear that Iran has never violated that agreement. They're signators to it. Now the United States violates it all the time—all the time. And so, when we put sanctions on them, who the hell are we to sanction anybody in the world? It's American arrogance and imperialism!

And so, when you look at Iran, we were able to bring along Europe, we were able to bring along the United Nations. When I was in Tehran, I went to the war museum and saw a United Nations resolution on the wall that said that Iran was the guilty party, and that Saddam Hussein was "our ally" in trying to punish them, because of the revolution that they had. And that they had the temerity to embarrass the superpower of the world for 444 days—that's something that's seared into the American psyche, and the reaction was this un-

Russian TV coverage of the Sept. 12, 2011 launching of Iran's Bushehr nuclear power plant—the first civilian nuclear power plant in Southwest Asia.

believable fear, and the unjust things we've done towards Iran.

Iran has never sought a nuclear weapon. And the day after the signature took place in Vienna, President Rouhani, the President, said finally, we've got an agreement that we won't have the bomb we never want to have anyway. The Ayatollah Khomeini, when the revolution took places, he put forth a *fatwa* twice, and the recent leader has got a *fatwa* out there also. Now, a *fatwa* is where the religious head interprets the Koran in its legal form. And so the *fatwa* is very simple: "We will not touch, or get involved, in weapons of mass destruction. We read the Koran that way."

And so if you look at this theocracy, which is what Iran is today, and you say, well, sure they want the bomb—they never did it, they never wanted it, and there's no intelligence organization in the world that has *any* evidence that they've sought the bomb! This is all a fabrication of Netanyahu 20 years ago, when he was telling us that they're going to have the bomb in a year, or two years. And he's been doing that, and it's been sanctioned in the American media, and the world media, accepting that Iran is this terrible, terrible country.

What is Unique about Man?

I've got to tell you, from what I've observed in Iran, it's second to none in terms of scientific accomplishment. What we've done for Iran with our sanctions, is make them the only independent nation in the world. They put up satellites. When you stand in downtown Tehran, you look around, you can count ten different derricks for building. And then you drive down the street, and it's traffic like New York. Now, for me, that's a sense of prosperity. And so to think that we've brought them to their knees, not at all. They obviously want to get their money back, the $150 billion; it's *their* money. And whenever you hear American leaders saying, "Well, it's terrible, they're going to go to war and they're going to spend this money; they're going to kill Americans,"—we kill Iranians!

So, it's really the American media, the American people are so uninformed about Persia. Persia is like China. They go back thousands of years in their contribution to human civilization, and when they say that Persia is anti-Semitic, it's ridiculous. One of the leaders of Persia, is the one who ended the Babylonian incarceration of the Jewish population, and brought them freedom. And you've got a Jewish community in Iran. And incidentally, there are Jews elected to the Parliament in Iran. So, to fabricate this situation is just ridiculous.

My words to you are, have no fear. The fact that they will now be recognized for what they are, as a very gifted people, with education. In Iran you have a situation where you go to school as a child, and you can go for a PhD at the end if you choose, and all of it's paid for by the government. They're just like the Chinese in this regard. They *value* teaching. And of course, the majority of the population of Iran is under 25.

Q: Hi, Lyn. It's A— here. On the calls we've been discussing the possibility in seeing breaks from Obama that can finally turn the tide, and remove him. The one that I'd read recently that I thought would be useful to bring up, is that I understand, there's an article that I read, that 50 NASA former astronauts and engineers have come out writing to the head of NASA, for them to change their position,—this greenie position,—on global warming, because indeed, we do see articles and so-called studies and things being done that support that fascist ideology. And what it seemed to me was, not really just to save NASA, but this represents to me another break from Obama, as the lead Greenie in the planet.

So, that that might be kind of an additional pile-on effect. And it seems that there are more and more people now that are finding the courage, whether it's in the in-

EIRNS/Ali Sharaf

The anti-nuclear Green policy is inherently Satanic. Here, an anti-nuclear demonstration in Germany in September 2009.

telligence community, or the scientific community, to display the kind of courage that the Senator did earlier in his career, at great risk to himself, not only from a professional or career standpoint, but right down to their very lives, as you and Helga have continued to demonstrate that. And so, we want to continue that break, and we want to demonstrate that same type of courage, as we come close to removing Obama. and I'd like to hear what you have to say on that.

LaRouche: I would say, mainly, the green policy is Satanic. It's inherently Satanic. Because just from the standpoint of the theological level, it's easy to make the case. What is the purpose, what is unique about mankind, that is not unique about the animals? It's that mankind is the only species we know of, which actually develops to a higher level, and whose development and progress in that development, defines his species.

This becomes a theological question, but it's also a scientific question. Mankind is the only species which is able to rise as a species from volition, from *volition*, and it's mankind's power of volition which makes this possible. And the green policy has always been a policy of genocide. It always was, and the policy of Obama is genocide, for example. And that's the issue.

The idea—people get confused about this religious issue. The point is, what is the difference between mankind and an animal? What's the difference? Therefore, if you define your species as human, what does that mean about your behavior? Your orientation in life? Your ambitions? Your devotions? What are they? Mankind is a unique species, and mankind has to behave like this unique species it is. And when you put a green policy into effect, you are actually—you're Satanic, actually. You're fairly described as a Satanic person. Because it's mankind's obligation to promote the species of mankind, in terms of—as Einstein did, in his own pragmatic way, he did exactly that. And he forced the elimination of what Bertrand Russell did.

Russell's Legacy

And what's the policy today that corresponds? Bertrand Russell's legacy. The British legacy, the British Empire's legacy. That's what evil is. And when people go against the obligation—and sometimes they're just innocent people; they don't really know what they're talking about, they don't know what the issue is—but they have a feeling about the issue. It comes like in family relationships. Families develop a sense of loyalty to the idea of the family: that they're supposed to create children, or help people to do the same thing, so that one generation is going to better than the next, will be better informed, will be a better achievement, will be a more advanced condition for mankind.

The typical thing is you get all kinds of great scientists. Kepler; Kepler discovered the Solar System. He discovered the Solar System; not by some mathematical magic, but he discovered it. Now we have a Galactic System, but the discovery of the Galactic System is a more powerful system and more urgent for the concerns of mankind, than even that system was.

And so therefore, mankind has a natural instinct built into mankind when it's not corrupted, to always ensure that the living generations are superior in their achievement to those that already lived. This used to be normal; I mean, the whole immigrants' process in the United States was full of that: the idea that better people are developed. How? By their own self-development, and by the means by which they're given access to that development.

Albert Einstein Society, Bern

The Twentieth Century's pre-eminent scientist, Albert Einstein, at Princeton in 1950.

And what Obama represents,—frankly this man is theologically and otherwise Satanic, period. [applause]

Q: It's been a challenge and I'm very honored to be working with you people for 20 years. I'm going to put my question out really quick, because otherwise I know I'm going to go too far; and then I'm going to footnote it a little bit. And the question is involved in my work with young people; particularly the 20-ish age group, young men and women, whom sometimes I interface with. And they get excited and they get interested; and they begin to talk among themselves and with me and with others about the ideas that we are talking about here, of course. And they go home, and they run into a hammer mill; and they get scared and they run away. And I kind of sense perhaps that their parents don't trust their own children's ability or necessity even to pursue these matters.

And I think of myself and the kind of things that I did, when I first met you people and I went out and I started talking about you; and this I'm going to say outright, it was in the Cornell University area. And I began to say after a while that there was something magic in your name. The reason for that is that if I got somebody to go into the Cornell or Ithaca community and talk about you, use your name and pursue your ideas, or question about you; that they would be sooner or later be attacked by somebody, who would be attacking their intelligence, their ability to reason. They'd kind of direct you to get out of the domain of intelligence and reasoning because you don't qualify. And of course, that's an insult.

And that's what I've been dedicated to; I've devoted my whole self to this policy for all my life, ever since I was in early school grades. I never accepted mathematics. I knew it was wrong from the beginning; that you cannot base a science on mathematics. And therefore you have to have an insight into those principles of discovery which were well known in earlier centuries; but which began to disappear during the course of the Twentieth Century and presently on.

And then I find these people, the next time I saw them, I could see in their eyes that they're mad as soon as they approach me; they're upset. So, I know what they've done; so I called that magic. And so, I think what I'm seeing with young people,—my question then is, how best to handle that, when I'm talking with these young people?

LaRouche: Well, let's give it a case. We had up until the Twentieth Century, the leading tendency in trans-European areas was to develop populations which had the equivalent of scientific abilities. What happened was, at the beginning of the Twentieth Century, there was a change. And the change was introduced chiefly by Bertrand Russell. And by that period, by the time that I was going to school, I was up against Satan, in fact; because that was what the policy was. The policy was that mathematics was the basis for reality. Now, mathematics is not the basis for reality; but people are hypnotized into believing that it is.

A Moment of Truth

Einstein was one of the people who was scolded because he didn't believe in these so-called practical forms of mathematics. And mathematics does not do anything for you, really, in terms of the advancement of the human species; it doesn't work.

And that's what I've been dedicated to; I've devoted my whole self to this policy for all my life, ever since I was in early school grades. I never accepted mathematics. I knew it was wrong from the beginning; that you cannot base a science on mathematics. And therefore you have to have an insight into those principles of discovery which were well known in earlier centuries; but which began to disappear during the course of the Twentieth Century and presently on. And therefore, the educational systems available to students in schools today, is almost genocide in one sense or the other.

Zepp-LaRouche: Well, this happens all over the world. If I look back for the last several decades of our organizing internationally, that particular phenome-non—what you are describing—is happening all the time. It happened to industrialists in Milan, who were told that if they don't stop working with us, their business will be destroyed. It happens to people in all ranges of—important people, less important people; and I can only say this was the same effort as demonizing Russia; as demonizing China.

And in a sense, this is the method. How do you prevent somebody from doing something different from what the establishment wants? You slander them, you say terrible things about them; you make it look as if something terrible happens to you if you don't quit working with these people. It works for a long time; because it induces a kind of fear. People are afraid that they're being dropped by their peer group, or something will happen to their career, or whatever.

Over the years, we have seen that the slanders are tailored to the specific group which is targeted. For example, if it's a trade unionist, they used to say—now no longer—"They are CIA." If it's an industrialist, they say, "Oh, they are KGB." If it's a Protestant, they say, "They are financed by the Vatican." And so forth and so on. So, they tailor the slanders to fit the fear-pattern of that particular group. And it works for a very long time; but I think now we have reached a point where it's what Lincoln identified: You can fool all the people some of the time, and some of the people all the time, but you cannot fool all the people all the time.

I think we have now reached a point where people realize that there is a moment of truth. So, you should just tell people that that's the method, and they shouldn't fall for it. In a certain sense, they have to make up their mind: do they want to be part of something which is clearly a destructive force, or do they want to be part of what is the solution? And only truth-seeking people will ever have the courage to stand up. So, you have to give up the idea that you can convince everybody; because people who are mediocre or cowards, you will not win them over. You can only do this to strengthen those who have the moral fiber to withstand tyranny.

A rocket installation in BRICS nation Brazil.

That's my answer. [applause]

Q: E—, native New Yorker; that's New York State, not New York City.

Europe has been unsuccessful at reproduction; but Islamic states from Indonesia to Morocco have been very successful at reproduction. Islamic nations have a long tradition of excellence in university education that is longer than the European university system. How can Europe best utilize resources from the Islamic world to rebuild its depleted workforce? That's my question.

Gravel: With a migration from the Middle East, in fact, that's the blessing in disguise. Because all of the countries that are being impacted have a problem of gentrification. Which is what made America great: It's not who is here, it's who came here and what they brought—and they don't all have to be educated. They just have to have the will to succeed. And whenever I hear a person like earlier, we had this person saying America's great, and it's the leaders,—well, that's really true. You get most of the immigrants who have a higher opinion of America than many Americans. And

this is understandable, because what they're living off of is the American values that were created much, much earlier, and are not being moving up to the top in terms of leadership.

A Vision of the Future

All of this with the exception that we Americans are a violent people; you know, what we did to the indigenous people of this continent, and then what we did with slavery, and now what we still see as the legacy of that. And when Nixon realized that "Hey, we can take the South from the Democrats; all we got to do is play to the white males." And that's what's going on in the Congress today; a lot of this Republican stuff is racist, rancid racism! I just want to add that to you.

Zepp-LaRouche: Well, I think it has to do with a question of a vison of the future. If people have the hope that there will be a future, they tend to like to procreate.

You have now in the United States in America, the first generation, the first time where people are satisfied with the fact that the coming generations will be worse off than the present ones. That has never existed in America's whole history; that's a completely new phenomenon. And I think that that is a sign of a dying society. And if people accept that it will go downhill, then it will go downhill.

So, my hope is that, I mean I have never believed, and there I agree with the Senator in what he said about the United States; I have always said I don't put the saving of Germany on Germany. I have always said I have to encircle Germany to crack it from the outside; through Russia, through China, through other developments. And I think that is exactly what is happening now; because the main center of development now is not Europe, and in a certain sense, it's also not the United States.

The center of development is the BRICS countries, is centered around China. And there is the growth, there is the momentum; that is where people have a future. Why do you think the BRICS countries have all a space program? Why do you think the Chinese have the most advanced space program? Because they are thinking about the next epoch of evolution. And I think what we want to do is, we want to rekindle—I mean, Germany, for example. It used to be called the "country of poets, thinkers, and inventors"; that is what we have to revive. That people have a pride about what they contributed and revive that. And then we'll talk about this tonight again. So please come tonight, because this is important.

I wouldn't look at it only as the Islamic world; because that in a certain sense is true, but it's also true for Africa. The Africans are also having lots of children. So I would look at it more from the standpoint of which countries have a vision of the future, because that what makes people want to build a family, want to be educated, want to study. If you think the world has come to an end, you may as well sit at home and pick your nose! [laughter]

Q: My first question is what kind of economic system are we trying to create, what kind of new paradigm is trying to be created? Is it going to be a system in which all of us as a collective are going to have power, and we're going to be leading the world as a collective? Or is it going to be a system in which I'm going to have an elite or a group of wealthy people making the rules for us?

Gravel: There are two elements to that. The first element is to solve the problem of poverty. It's a little bit like, you can't be reflective and mature if you don't have enough food to eat; that's what's going to command your intelligence. So the first step—and that's the reason why the Chinese "One Belt, One Road" is going to be so significant—is because of the prosperity it will bring to all of these areas. Not at the point of a gun, but as a point of personal need and success.

And so that's the first stage. And once you arrive at that stage where you can now reflect, you can mature, and that's where education comes in. And so when you want to see the countries that are moving ahead and that are going to be the leaders of tomorrow, just look at what countries are providing the most education to their young; and it's *not* the United States, it's *not* the United States. And that's the sadness of it, because we're squandering our wealth on a culture of militarism, and I don't see—I'm just not optimistic in that regard. And that's the reason why in my earlier comments I was looking to—I want a solution, too! Very much! And that solution, I see coming is from China and the BRICS. And so those are the two stages that I feel in responding to your question.

Speed: Do you want to respond to that?

What is Education?

LaRouche: No, that's a perfectly fine answer.

Q: [follow-up] Now, the other question I have is if there was another way as a collective that we all could free ourselves from the,—because you know the system we have been living in since thousands of years, the people in power have kept all this knowledge from us, and only they have the knowledge and the power, and they keep us ignorant. If we do have this knowledge, we would realize that eventually we don't really need an elite to be telling us what to do or what we cannot do, you see? Like, for example, there is a way the rich people make their money; and we can learn eventually, as a collective, how to make money too. How to build wealth.

Now, my question is, are the Chinese and Russians willing to make knowledge available for everybody? Are they going to disclose the file—because there is so much that has been hidden from us, and not only the United States, but a lot of world leaders know about a lot of stuff.

Now, are they willing to disclose this file, disclose, for example, something of the extraterrestrial phenomena? I know to a lot of people it might sound crazy, but at this point, there are so many proofs of so many sightings of this phenomenon, that I do believe that a lot of world leaders know about it, and they're just keeping it from us. Are they willing to disclose these files?

Speed: If you just asked a question, we should answer, because there's other people …

Q: [follow-up] OK, that's fine.

LaRouche: There are problems here in what your question is, and that's what stymies some of us to some degree. Education is not something which is delivered, as by a recipe. And so you're not be denied the recipe. Because the development of the human mind comes from childhood, and it comes from the development of childhood in understanding what is wrong or right about what education is.

And there've been a few heavy survivors in the history of science, real heavy survivors, but they've been limited in number. Most people have a mixture of something they learned, not necessarily science, but they have gained what we call skill. And the distinction of skill, is that it's something you can pass on to other people and show them the tricks that will do something, help them to understand how they might find a trick. But the idea that you can sort of "deliver" education, *per se*,—it's not possible. It's the self-development of

EIRNS/Philip Ulanowsky

"It's self-development of the individual mind, which is the foundation of true education."

the individual mind, which is the foundation of true education: *self*-development, not being instructed from the outside but *self*-development, and seeking out people who will give you access to what you use as *self*-development.

So the principle is not some idea of the greedy people are holding back any facts. But the fact is, the educational system has gone down, consistently, over the entire period since the beginning of the Twentieth Century. In the Twentieth Century, education in general was dominated by one person, Bertrand Russell, and Bertrand Russell's policy determined the education of *scientists*. And the incompetence introduced to the factors of science, has been the major problem; it's been the thing I've made my career out of, of attacking this crap, that the stuff that's practical is important.

Because if you don't have a discovery *by yourself*, if you haven't worked it out by yourself, you don't know it. And the point you want to do is to stimulate people,—like children, you want to stimulate them to make discoveries, true discoveries, which are discoveries on their part. You want to stimulate them by asking the right questions. And the secret of education is asking children the right questions. And you should have all the information and gadgets and so forth around it, to help them struggle through that question. [applause]

Speed: That's nice!

Q: Happy birthday! Sorry I was a little bit late, but I'm very pleased to be able to wish you happy birthday. I also wanted to take a minute to ask you a question, and also to Helga; and to also thank you for your relentless attack on reductionism for the last 40 years that I've known you. Because it's always been a breath of fresh air, and I grew up in an educational system where we were taught to dot our t's and cross our i's, and all kinds of things that were backwards. And when I ran into people who had been in dialogue with you and they were saying, "Wait a minute, is that really the way it works? What do you think? Does it work that way, or the opposite?"

Derivatives

It's like Euclid, the attacks on Euclid that we've made as a movement; it's based on this relentless attack on reductionism as a mentality instead of embracing of universal principle. And there can't be any education that doesn't put universal principles front and center. And that's why our scientific education has failed, because that's totally left out. You know, you've got a bunch of engineers that can put a man on the Moon, but they can't figure out that killing people for no reason with napalm is *wrong*! There's something wrong with their scientific education, when they have that kind of an inability to understand humanity. So I just want to thank you for that.

And Helga, I think what you've tried to do in conceptualizing the Schiller Institute, it's so valuable to us—and we want to create a sea change in the world around the discoveries of what—we have some wonderful things to spread the news about today, about what the BRICS are doing, and what the future is, what we can accomplish; and we have a population that has withdrawn from reality because they don't trust the news any more, and they're right about that. But they don't realize that they can discover the truth on their own.

So this is the nut we have to crack. And as you were saying about Germany, where it was destroyed, it was targetted precisely because it was the center of a Renaissance quality, with Bach and Beethoven and Riemann, and the great artists, and Schiller; this was why Germany was attacked. It's also why the United States was attacked in the postwar period,—we didn't have that quality but the kernel of this was still alive here.

FIGURE 1
OTC Foreign Exchange Derivatives
$ trillions, notional principal by currency

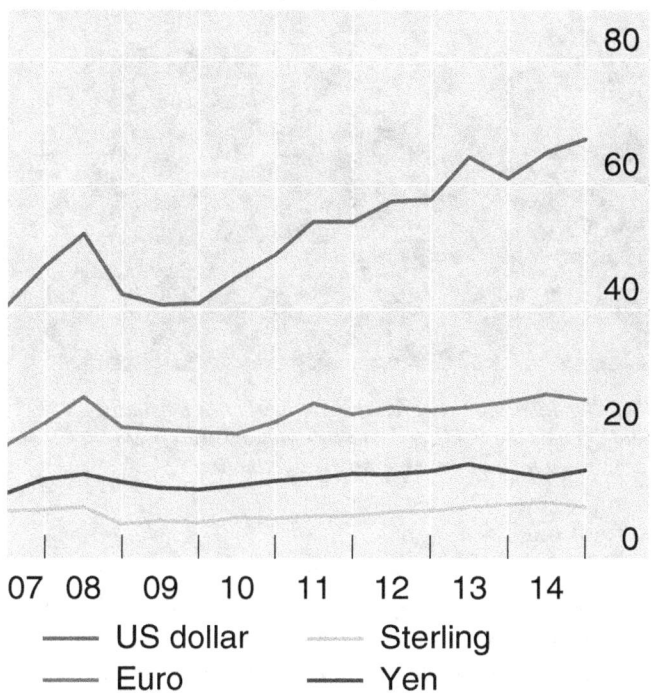

— US dollar   ‑‑‑‑ Sterling
— Euro   — Yen

This BIS chart, published in its September 2015 Quarterly Report, shows the dramatic growth of dollar-denominated foreign exchange derivatives (i.e. unpayable gambling debts) since 2007-8.

And we've got to keep that alive and revive this.

And my question is, what do you think we should do next, to revive and to create a mass movement for development in this country, which means to recover our wits about what our country is dedicated to? And you've already done a lot, but maybe you can throw out some more ideas.

Zepp-LaRouche: I can give you a very short answer: Go out into the whole world and multiply. [LaRouche laughs] Go out into the world and multiply! [applause]

Q: Hello, Mr. LaRouche, and thank you for the knowledge and the insights that you give us in these sessions. I really appreciate that a lot, so thank you for that.

I have a question and it's on derivatives. When I was reading about it the past week, I finally got an explanation that made sense. Usually it's just explained as "It's too difficult to explain," and it's left at that. Now, they mention is being something like an insurance contract, so when it comes to term and expires, it's done. But you're hedging on a loss that you hope doesn't happen. So I just wonder, what's the cultural problem that allows derivatives and other forms of gambling hedges to be seen as economic wealth, and I would like to address this to the Schiller Institute, and in particular to Helga, if you're able to explain that?

Zepp-LaRouche: Well, originally, it was legitimate that you would take out insurance on business in the future, so that you think, let's say, in three months, I will buy something, and I want to make sure the currency doesn't collapse in the mean time, so there was a certain rationale in saying I will take insurance on that, so that I'm covered and don't have a total loss. Like also a ship, in even earlier times: you would take insurance that the ship arrives in time with the cargo for some contract you made maybe a year earlier.

But then, in a certain sense, that became a thing in itself, so people would bet on the insurance, and then bet on the bet, and bet on the bet, and bet on the bet, and this became so complicated, that these things become completely divorced from the actual, physical economy. And the whole derivatives market by now is a complete fantasy, because there is absolutely no correlation any more between real production and these derivatives. So you have a situation where the total outstanding derivatives, according to our best estimate, is $2 quadrillion! That's about ten times the GDP of the world.

A Credit System

And therefore, this system is hopelessly bankrupt, because they did the bailouts after 2008,—you know, quantitative easing, bailouts, all these measures. Then they came to the conclusion that you cannot continue to do that, and they started to invent the "bail-in." Now, both the United States and all European countries have a bail-in law, which is the Cyprus model. And if you look at the EU legislation which made this bail-in law, which means basically confiscation of all the accounts of people who have either private accounts or business accounts, you just cut it in half, or you cut 60%, you take all of it away: That's bail-in.

When we did this work many years ago, I looked at who came up with this idea, and it was something called ISDA [International Swaps and Derivatives Association], which is short for an organization which consists of the 28 largest banks in the world. So the EU Commission went to the 28 largest banks in the world and had them make a law for a bail-in, in case of some bankruptcy.

So, you can go to the wolf and say, "protect the chickens;" you know, that's the same thing!

In a certain sense, if now this event happens, which you know, several people have joined Lyn in saying that it could happen any moment; it could be triggered by a Grexit, it could be triggered by one big bank failing; if this bail-in mechanism were implemented, it would probably cover only 1% of all existing accounts. Because the outstanding derivatives are so much bigger, there is no way,—you know, in a certain sense, this is why what these governments are doing is really criminal! All of them know that this system is bankrupt, because they have probably even more detailed data than we have, because they can collect the central bank data. So for them to drive this in the way they are doing, they are gambling with the lives of billions of people. So the derivatives are completely unnecessary. We should eliminate them. I mean, the idea,—people who say that you need derivatives, it's a complete lie, you don't need them.

Schiller Institute

The evening session of the Sept. 12 Schiller Institute event featured a number of musical presentations. Kicking off the proceedings was the Schiller Institute chorus's presentation of some sections of Bach's Jesu Meine Freude, shown here. John Sigerson is conducting.

What you need is a credit system, which is basically a system of sovereign countries having national banks, and there must be some kind of a clearing agency inbetween, because you want to have long-term trade, you want to have long-term international investment, and there must be some kind of accounting way of balancing the differences; some countries are rich with raw materials, some have no raw materials; some countries are big, some are small; and you have to balance that somehow. And for that, you need an international clearing agency, which calculates these balances, and you don't want to have monetarism sneak back in. Therefore you have to look at the real economy, the increase of productivity, as the only measurement. Because you want to have 10-year investment, 20-year investment, and to have a credit system is relatively easy: You don't need derivatives.

You have to get rid of this entire philosophy of money making money. Money doesn't make money! I mean, I have never seen a dollar shovelling a shovel or something.

No, I think we need to go back to a system of real production, of the measurement being the increase of the productivity of the population, and everything should be subsumed by that. So the earlier questioner was asking, what is the new paradigm, or the new society going to be? I think that we will only come out of this as a human civilization if we replace the present thinking about money. Phenomena like Trump should be renamed from Trump to Dump; and we should have a dumping system for trumping. [laughter]

We will only come out of this if there is a completely different idea that what human creativity can produce in terms of science, in terms of art. That is what makes a human life livable. And that will become the dominant philosophy. In a certain sense China is the closest country to doing that, with their meritocracy. And they're trying to move very quickly to eliminate remnants of corruption from the past; they're moving to eliminate the speculation bubble, which had built up around Shanghai and Hongkong, and I think that that will be in a certain sense, a beacon for the world how to go. And I'm saying this, in this hotel. [laughter]

Q: This is R— from Bergen County, New Jersey. I'd like to address my question to Helga. I'm very disturbed about a lot of the activities that had been going on under the Bush and Obama administration, that I think can only be characterized as criminal. I'm talking about war crimes, I'm talking about atrocities.

For example, in the recent refugee crisis, LPAC is

the only organization that I know of that has actually traced the origins of the refugee crisis to the activities of the Obama administration in bombing Libya, executing its leader, and creating God-only-knows what kind of chaos within that country. I also have not noticed in the press any kind of tangible description of what is really going on in Libya, that would cause people to risk a horrendous death to get out of it. That seems to have been blacked out.

Nuremberg Trials

So it seems to me, we're talking about major war crimes, murder.

Now, I'm under the impression that murder is considered to be a crime; and because Americans aren't raising enough of a ruckus about it, the longer that it is allowed to happen, the more it becomes legitimized. And people go around thinking, "Yeah, we can kill anybody we want, because we do it, right?" Now, in Germany I know you had Nuremberg Trials, and so my question to you is, what was the point of the Nuremberg Trials, and what effect did it have on Germans at that time?

And secondly, do we not need a Nuremberg Tribunal at some point to completely purge ourselves of the evil that is going on, and has been going on for the last 100 years, with regard to the U.S.?

Zepp-LaRouche: I think that concerning the German side of it, unlike Japan, Germany has reviewed its crimes, and I think that there is a very strong impulse that the vast, vast, vast majority of Germans never want war again. The reason why Schröder went against the Iraq War, and why the government went against the Libya war and did not participate in it, despite massive U.S. pressure to do so, is because, I think the German population had, between the experience of two world wars fought on its soil, and a recognition that the Nazis were about the deepest you could fall, that I think there is a genuine desire, never, ever to have war again. And in a certain sense, that is one of the stronger qualities which I think play in the present situation right now.

Now, concerning the second part of your question: I mean, the Nuremberg Tribunal Statutes say that to prepare a war of aggression is already a war crime, and by that standard, well, the people who are playing around with a first-strike policy with the implicit intention that you could win a thermonuclear war, in my view, fulfill that question of a war crime already.

And obviously, in order to enforce that, you need somebody to do it. It's not enough to state it, but you need some authority to do that, and I think the only people who could do that are the American people. I do not expect the United Nations to do; I don't expect anybody else to do it.

But in a certain sense, it's like what happened with Germany, the country which was at one point, in my humble opinion, really the most advanced culture: Because in the period of the German Classic you had the most lofty ideal of humanity ever; if you look at the writings of people like Schiller, or the music of Bach, Beethoven, and others; there is no higher expression of the beauty of the human being than that. And with the Humboldt education system, Germany came very close to making that the universal principle to mediate that image of man to the whole society.

So from that standpoint, to drop that deeply, as the Nazis did,—then the question is, why did the German people not resist more? Now one thing one can say, is, it was not so clear what Hitler would become—I mean, that's the only apology one can say, that it only became gradually clear. But then you had this complex geopolitical situation, where Hitler was financed from abroad; I'm not saying the Germans did not also support him, but without Montagu Norman, without Prescott Bush, without Averell Harriman, who knows if Hitler would have made it?

So then, we see how people get accustomed, how they adapt. In the beginning, there was a stronger resistance; then, as the majority was backing Hitler and you had the different pogroms and elimination of opposition, people adapted more and more and more! I think the same process is going on in the United States; people look at it, and then, you know, you get used to what you're seeing! That is something you have to recognize and wake people up.

But, in my view, to prepare a war of aggression, including the use of nuclear weapons, including the threat or the risk that that may lead to the extinction of civilization, I think that is a war crime. And people better start to think about that, because you know, I think that that is a moral challenge for the American people.

Gravel: [audio loss] If I'd to add to that, just in pure hindsight . . . .

Moving Now to Prevent War

Here, there's hope. Watch what's going on in Britain right now. There's a group that wants to use the same legal vehicle they did with Pinochet, and try to arrest and hold Netanyahu as a war criminal for what's happened; and are using the fact that some of the people killed in Gaza were of British citizenship.

The answer's real simple. It's the Treaty of Rome, which the United States has not bought into, but keep in mind, we also had the situation in Spain; the reason why Henry Kissinger can't travel to Europe is because the Spanish judge tried to catch him, and he was spirited out of Paris overnight for fear of arrest. So, it's

---

We have, with the United Nations meeting coming in the course of this next week,—this thing by itself can be the instrument for preventing thermonuclear war. Now this is not an isolated matter; it's complicated, but life is always complicated in the main. It's that what has happened is that Obama has lost trend, he has lost footing, and he's hanging out there, and what happened was that Putin fooled him. It was not any bad fooling business, but simply what Putin did has screwed up, as we say, the kind of plan that Obama was committed to.

---

closing in on these criminals. And those criminals include American Presidents and Vice Presidents.

Zepp-LaRouche: And also I should add that Jeremy Corbyn who was voted in today [as leader of Britain's Labour Party] not only wants to implement Glass-Steagall; he wants to put Tony Blair before a war crimes tribunal. And he wants to abolish the Monarchy! [applause]

Q: My name is S— I've been very active with Mr. LaRouche's campaigns before, as well as with Mr. Ramsey Clark: They are the two men who I think the whole world have entrusted them with some hope. I stopped attending any functions after the crazy things happened in 9/11 and whatever commotion in the world came afterwards, but finally, when [Schiller Institute organizer] Angela Vullo sent me this email telling me about your new campaign for peace, I thank you both for bringing the blood back into my body. I'm running for Senate for the Parliament of Egypt, and I will definitely do my best to connect both of you and this movement with the Egyptian people. I thank you *very* much! And I'm just thrilled. Thank so very much, and thank you, Mrs. LaRouche. [applause]

Q: Good afternoon, Mr. LaRouche, R— from

Brooklyn. You were discussing on the Thursday night call [Fireside Chat] about Putin taking a tactic that would outflank Obama, and the fact that this would perhaps be a preventative to nuclear confrontation. One of the things that was I was thinking of asking, do you foresee any future tactics that would help in this area, to keep the United States and Russia from having a nuclear exchange?

LaRouche: OK, fine: Yes, I do have a view on this thing. What I've mentioned in the opening of this event today, is, the fact is that we have, with the United Nations meeting coming in the course of this next week,—this thing by itself can be the instrument for preventing thermonuclear war. Now this is not an isolated matter; it's complicated, but life is always complicated in the main. It's that what has happened is that Obama has lost trend, he has lost footing, and he's hanging out there, and what happened was that Putin fooled him. It was not any bad fooling business, but simply what Putin did has screwed up, as we say, the kind of plan that Obama was committed to.

He was concentrating on going directly into the center of Europe and areas like that into fringes, spreading things as had been done before, which Obama had done; Obama was a prophet of this kind of thing especially. Dick Cheney was a comparable figure, but Cheney is mild compared to Obama.

So the point has come that this thing got jammed up. You saw a change, first of all,—I picked up the change in Russia, on the events that were developing in Russia, that something was happening. What happened with China [their Sept 3 Victory parade], which was organized largely in coordination with Putin; Putin was a big organizer of this thing. Then I saw what was happening next, and Putin made a smart move, which by his methods outflanked Obama.

So now, what happens, this means we have an enhanced opportunity to rid ourselves of the Obama pestilence by concentrating on support, appropriate forms of support, for the United Nations meeting which is coming up now during this month. This is the best option we have now, for a peaceful solution, for this crisis now.

> This means we have an enhanced opportunity to rid ourselves of the Obama pestilence by concentrating on support, appropriate forms of support for the United Nations meeting which is coming up now during this month. This is the best option we have now, for a peaceful solution for this crisis now. It can work. Look at the facts of the matter; look at what China represents. Now look at what India represents, combined with that. Look at some other locations on the planet. Look at the BRICS movement in general. All of these forces are converging, whether they're fully witting or not, in a direction to what? Avoid thermonuclear war. But at the same time, eliminate the agency which would launch the thermonuclear war.

It can work. Look at the facts of the matter; look at what China represents. Now look at what India represents, combined with that. Look at some other locations on the planet. Look at the BRICS movement in general. All of these forces are converging, whether they're fully witting or not, in a direction to what? *Avoid thermonuclear war.* But at the same time, eliminate the agency which would launch the thermonuclear war.

Leaders with Courage

We saw this in Germany. We saw this change in Germany in the way the refugee population was being handled. And Germany decided to make that move; that was a highly moral move. It was a unique one. Now, Germany was the first nation outside of Russia, in a sense, to make that kind of step. And what happened, parts of the United States were trembling out of guilt; Wall Street is trembling, because Wall Street knows it cannot survive! It wants all kinds of terror.

Now what is happening in the coming week and beyond, and what is implicit now at this time, because it's coming on: The time has come, that it is possible, it is feasible, to dump Obama one way or the other, and to end this plan of major war which we've been discussing here so far; we've been discussing around those same areas.

Therefore, this is the moment, the greatest opportunity of moment, now placed on the desk before us right now. This may not be the final solution; this may not be the answer. But it's an indication the answer is possible now. And the best shot we have, is going to be by influencing the people in the United States and other countries, around the United Nations event now, and next week. This is the best option in sight right now, considering what I've already referenced there. These are the best options available.

And we should just go like tigers, and get this thing moving: integrate everything with what this United Nations event is. Push it for all it's worth. It's the best instrument because we see that many parts of the planet *don't want that kind of war.* And that's the best shot we have available to us right now.

Speed: So we're going to ask now for summary remarks from Helga, Senator Gravel and then from Lyn.

Zepp-LaRouche: I think what Lyn just said is what

> The time has come, that it is possible, it is feasible, to dump Obama one way or the other, and to end this plan of major war which we've been discussing here so far; we've been discussing around those same areas. And therefore, this is the moment, the greatest opportunity of moment, now placed on the desk before us, right now. This may not be the final solution; this may not be the answer. But it's an indication the answer is possible now. And this is the best shot we have, is going to be by influencing the people in the United States and other countries, around the United Nations event now, and next week. This is the best option in sight, right now, considering what I've already referenced there. These are the best options available.

I would to underline. Because there will be an extraordinary combination of world leaders all being aware of the dangers, and if you can help us in the next days, I think the actual United Nations process will go on, with the top leadership being there until Oct. 6, so that is a window of three weeks. And I don't know exactly when who will speak, but there will be a special session on refugees; there will be a special session on climate change that we should not forget, even if that's not the main focus.

But we produced this new report, that climate change is not science but depopulation. You should absolutely get this report, read it, and also distribute it as much as you can to the embassies, to institutions. There are many institutions in New York which have headquarters here. We can really have a major, major impact right here in New York, in Manhattan.

And I think the more people who would join this idea, you know, I wrote this appeal to the governments to use this UN General Assembly to really address the issue, and anybody can address this forum. Remember, many years ago, [then Guyana Foreign Minister] Fred Wills used this exact platform to bring in the question of the just new world economic order; so any representative from any country—it can be a small country; the smallest country can bring into this platform the need to move to the World Land-Bridge. If we get one leader to say, "we need the World Land-Bridge as a program for reconstruction," I think the genie would be out of the bottle forever!

So, I think all we need is one, hopefully more, leader who addresses the issue the way we do. They don't have to use our words, because everybody has their own style and way; but somebody has to say that the system is bankrupt, that we are approaching World War III, and we need a global program of reconstruction which allows the survival of all human beings on this planet. And that there is a program that the BRICS countries and the Chinese have offered, the "win-win" policy, and there is a demand that all the governments respond to that in a positive way.

So if any one leader would say that, and make a motion in front of the world public, I think everybody would agree! But what is required is that one country or a group of countries has the courage to do that. And we can help to create an environment so that could take place. So that is what I would say you should concentrate on with all your force for the next days and two, three weeks.

Release the 28 Pages

Gravel: I would associated myself with her remarks, period. So I can't add anything to that.

I would just add, that one of the issues that's perking within the Congress, is, of course, the release of the 28 pages [of the Joint Congressional Inquiry on 9/11]. And that situation I characterize, and I'm ashamed to say it: it's truly ridiculous; it's a ridiculous issue. Because the Congress is the one that classified it, and therefore, they can un-classify it. But what they want to do is do it through a legislative process. Well, my court case in 1972, where the Supreme Court ruled that whatever I did, or whatever any member of Congress would do, in releasing classified information, he could not be detained in any other locale. And this is in the Constitution: It's the "speech and debate clause" of the Constitution.

And so what we need, and I've already been approached and I'll be going to Washington to try to help out, but what we need is for *any single member* to release those papers, the 28 pages. But here again, it's the Congress itself that's bound itself by this element of secrecy that really doesn't exist! It's a figment of their imagination! And that, of course, is what's destroying our democracy.

Sakharov made what I thought was a very perceptive statement. He said what brought down the Soviet Union was not missiles, was not weaponry; what brought down the Soviet Union was the dismemberment of the elements of secrecy which denied the Russian people the knowledge of what was going on. This is called *perestroika*; *perestroika* and *glasnost*. And that's what caused the implosion.

Now what we need to do is have a similar implosion in the United States, where any one member of Congress would stand up and release—there's no threat! There's *no legal threat* to that person, and that's what the case had been all about in 1972. And of course, *no* one has done anything since '72 to utilize the principle in the Constitution, now unanimously approved by the Supreme Court of the United States, and in subsequent case law.

And so, hopefully that would change, and be somewhat of a revelation to the American public, because there's so much attention being focussed on the 28 pages. I can tell you what's in it. It's just the financing that was going on through the Wahhabist movement within Saudi Arabia; this is no secret. It's been going on for decades and decades, and that's what's created the extreme elements of Islam. And so it was funded by the leadership, whether it was organized or not, it was just the de facto leadership; in fact, the King in Saudi Arabia is very limited as to what he can do, because of this climate of supporting Wahhabism financially throughout the Kingdom.

So, let's hope that there's a change that takes place in Congress. It would accelerate other facets of this; and I will certainly try to bring to my audience at the UN on Monday the message we have from the *EIR* and the answer from my perspective. I know that from your organization, you feel that the answer is in the United States. Unfortunately, I'm ashamed to say, I've given up on that score; I think the answer is with the other countries coming in, and China and Russia will save us from ourselves.

Thank you.

LaRouche: I'm alive as usual. I would pick on the same thing that he just presented. It's the same issue. But just autobiographically: I went through this process, which led into 9/11; at that point, I was concentrating on some evidence which we had from certain parties in the British Empire, in Manhattan. And I was then informed, more or less, with all of the kinds of evidence which indicated what 9/11 would become; in other words, I didn't exactly how it would happen, but I knew all the evidence of how it was organized, and I still have that knowledge.

So the point now is that Obama is defending this policy, this crime. And we have now a new meeting in Manhattan [the United Nations General Assembly], a great meeting in Manhattan, an international meeting in Manhattan. I think the time has come, to break that privilege which had been taken to hide everything about 9/11 so-called.

I know what the evidence was that was leading

EIRNS

A revolutionary change occurred globally when Guyanese Foreign Minister Fred Wills addressed the UN General Assembly on Sept. 8, 1976, and called for replacing the IMF with "international development banks."

into 9/11. I knew it was the British Empire; I knew it was a special committee organized by the British offshore, of the oil provisions, the oil games, I knew that! I'd been doing also some work in Germany in terms of investigating certain areas. But I knew a certain number of members of the press, in Germany, who shared the information that I had. And we have some other members of our organization in the United States, as well as abroad—we know every important fact required, and sufficient to throw Obama out of office, for his continued efforts in defense of what happened in Manhattan and elsewhere.

This is the operation, and every member of Congress who lacks the guts to come forth and state that information, who had that information as such, is really guilty. And the time has come for them to confess their guilt and say, I'm holding evidence, which would force the United States to hold the guilty responsible. I myself knew every bit of the information needed, and I have other persons who, like me, knew that information. And I was there, one time, by video means, to see the planes which had been captured by the Saudi agents who actually destroyed people in the 9/11 operation.

This is a crime. We know who did it. We know what kinds of people did it. And that has been suppressed. I think that that issue is very important as a weapon, because some of us have known the actual facts, by personal knowledge of what was behind this. But the powers that be said "No, you can't say that." And a lot people said, "No, you can't say that." But it always was true. It's still true today. Right now, it's still true.

And that is the way we can get the United States and its honor back again. [applause]

Speed: That concludes our session. And we're now going to take a break.

And we should just go like tigers, and get this thing moving: integrate everything with what this United Nations event is. Push it for all it's worth. It's the best instrument, because we see that many parts of the planet don't want that kind of war. And that's the best shot we have available to us right now.

Every Day Counts In Today's Showdown To Save Civilization

That's why you need EIR's **Daily Alert Service**, a strategic overview compiled with the input of Lyndon LaRouche, and delivered to your email 5 days a week.

For example: On Sept. 30 EIR's Daily Alert featured Lyndon LaRouche's warning that the action must be taken immediately to remove President Obama in order to not only avoid further provocations toward World War III, but to avoid a disorderly collapse of Wall Street.

"If Wall Street collapses in a debt panic, that chaotic destructive force can lead to death and destruction in the United States and around the world," he said. FDR's Glass-Steagall is needed now.

Russian President Vladimir Putin's recent initiative in Syria has weakened Obama and created the necessary opening to do what's needed. But time is of the essence.

This is intelligence you need to act on, if we are going to survive as a nation and a species. Can you really afford to be without it?

THURSDAY, OCTOBER 1, 2015

EIR Daily Alert Service

EIR DAILY ALERT SERVICE P.O. BOX 17390, WASHINGTON, DC 20041-0390

- LaRouche: Wall Street Must Be Shut Down Before It Crashes
- Kerry Confirms Shift in U.S. Policy on Syria, Assad
- Putin Orders First Air Strikes Against Syrian Jihadists
- Russia's Upper House Approves Use of Armed Forces Abroad
- German Government Rejects Turkish Proposal for 'Safe Zones' in Syria
- Senator Warren: Glass-Steagall 'Is Exactly What We Should Do'
- German Saving Banks Threatened by Zero Rates Policy and EU Over-Regulation
- Senator Feinstein Thinks Russia's Move in Syria May Be Positive
- Dana Rohrabacher, Chair, House Subcommittee on Europe, Eurasia, and Emerging Threats, Holds Hearing on Terrorist Threat in Russia
- Rep. Dana Rohrabacher Attacks U.S. Support of Saudis, and Campaign To Overthrow Assad in House Foreign Affairs Committee
- BRICS Foreign Ministers Meet in New York
- NASA May Join Chinese/European Space Science Mission
- Finding Water on Mars Provokes Broad Debate in China
- Secretary John Kerry Reviews the 2013 Powerful Example of Cooperating with

---

A Universe in the very small

by Liona Fan-Chiang

Sept. 13—The past few years have seen the news peppered with articles about the sub-subatomic: elementary particles, more elementary than protons or neutrons, that make up everything. These particles have only been able to be studied under extreme conditions, where energies equivalent to a million billion degrees are looked down upon as too weak.

So where do those plain old protons and neutrons that nuclear engineers work with fit in? What about that big table of isotopes ordered by neutron and proton number? Are they so well-understood and completely figured out that there's nothing else to learn from these old-fashioned friends? Despite the idea that protons, neutrons, and electrons are not that special, it is they that determine chemistry, nuclear energy, and nuclear medicine, at least on Earth.

In fact, in these relatively low-energy domains (at least 1000 times less energetic than the energy required to investigate sub-atomic particles), there are still many standing paradoxes, some almost a millennium old. Many of these are discussed in detail in Norman Cook's book *Models of the Atomic Nucleus* (second edition, Springer, 2010). I want to point out just a few.

Finding a Model

Perhaps the clearest sign that the domain of nuclear physics is not all figured out, is the fact that not just several, but more than 30 different models are applied to explain different aspects of the nucleus. They can be broadly classified into three or four, but all of them have stayed around to some extent because each has been able to explain some part of the experimental data, although not one of them accounts for it all. Is the nucleus like a liquid, solid or gas? Or is it akin to the quantum mechanical electron cloud?

For example: The nucleus modeled as a liquid drop has been used, with some corrections, to calculate the binding energy, which is related to how much energy will come out of a nuclear reaction. The actual values have been gathered from experiments from the 1930s-50s. The reason for the values has not been that clear. The model which has most accurately accounted for the curve has been the liquid-drop model. This model, however, does not account for another very well-known characteristic of nuclear reactions.

Nuclear fission, the splitting of one atom into two or more, almost always occurs asymmetrically. That is, the two pieces that a large nucleus like uranium breaks up into, are almost always a large and a small piece, and not two nearly equal pieces (**Figures 2 and 3**). The liquid drop, and many other models, can be massaged into giving asymmetric pieces but do not account for the fact that fission occurs primarily asymmetrically. For this, Cook proposes his crystalline lattice model. Another curious aspect of the distribution of fission fragments of various nuclei is that the larger nucleus is always centered around 132-140 nucleons, while the smaller seems to adjust to maintain an approximately 2:3 proportion. What is so preferable about this nucleon number? That remains unexplained.

FIGURE 1

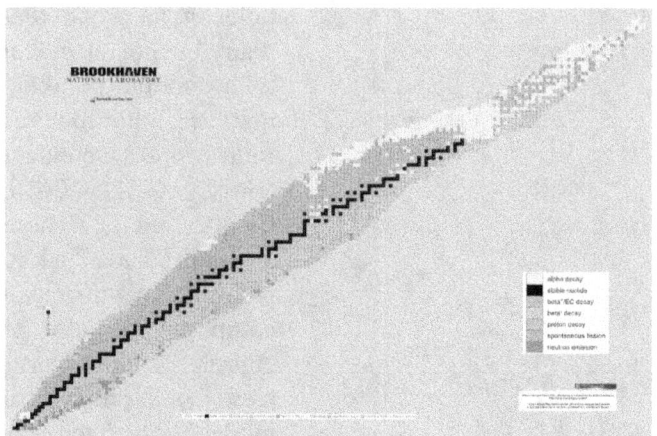

Brookhaven National Lab

Chart of all nuclei organized by number of protons (y-axis) and number of neutrons (x-axis). The colors represent decay modes, i.e. particles emitted when the nucleus decays.

FIGURE 2

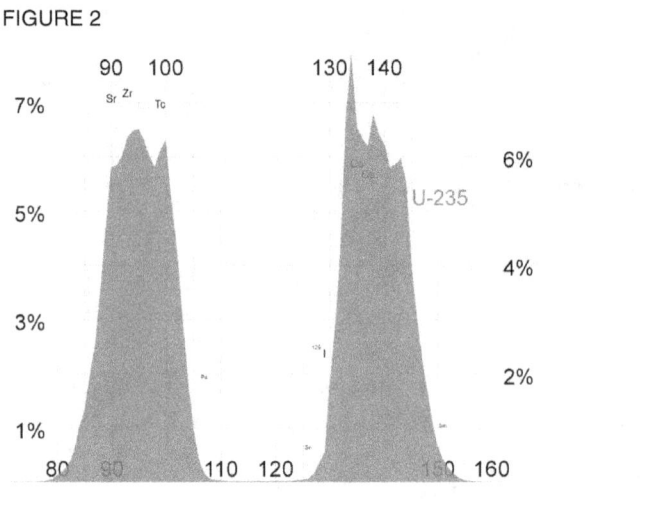

Fission products (before decay) of uranium-235. If the decay products were the same size, this curve would be one hump centered around 117. The x-axis is atomic mass units (number of protons plus neutrons).

FIGURE 3

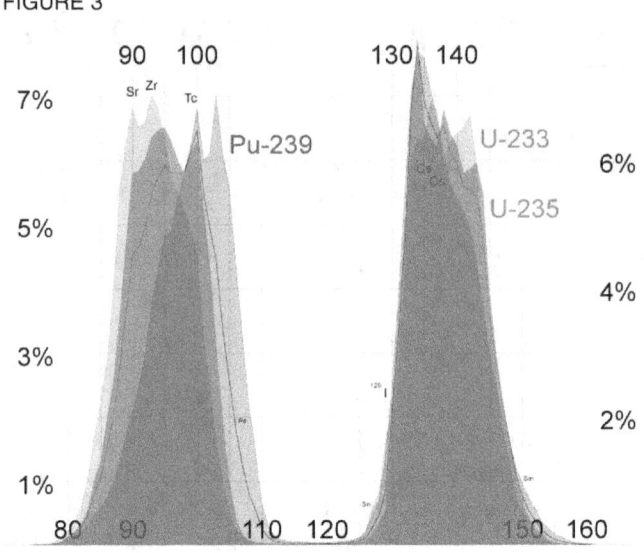

wikipedia user JWB

Fission products (before decay) of uranium-235, uranium-233, and plutonium-239. Notice that the larger piece centers around 140 atomic mass units for all three.

Here is another basic property, studied since the beginning of nuclear science. Natural radioactive decay occurs by three modes: alpha, beta+, and beta-. Beta+ and beta- are positively and negatively charged electrons. Alpha radiation is composed of helium nuclei: two protons and two neutrons. A chart of all nuclei and their decay modes makes the natural tendency for transition clear (**Figure 1**). The black are stable nuclei. Above the line of stable nuclides, atoms lose a positive electron, and therefore a positive charge, becoming an element lower in the periodic table and also moving closer toward stability.

Below the line of stable nuclides, nuclei tend toward the opposite route, losing a negative charge, thereby creating extra positive charge, and becoming an element one higher in the periodic table. The next most common form of decay is alpha radiation (shaded yellow in the diagram). This is the decay output of uranium for example. Aside from these, there are a few nuclei which release protons or neutrons, but almost all of such nuclei live for less than a millisecond.

Why would an atom release an entire cluster of two protons and two neutrons, and not just a single one of either? Other related data include the fact that the helium nucleus appears to be smaller than expected for the number of particles it has, and that many, but not all, nuclei with atomic numbers that are multiples of four, are abundant (He-4, C-12, O-16, Ca-40, etc.). These anomalies have led to many models of nuclei composed partially or entirely of alpha particles. Cook proposes a model in which the core and the outliers are alpha particles.

A more recent body

FIGURE 4

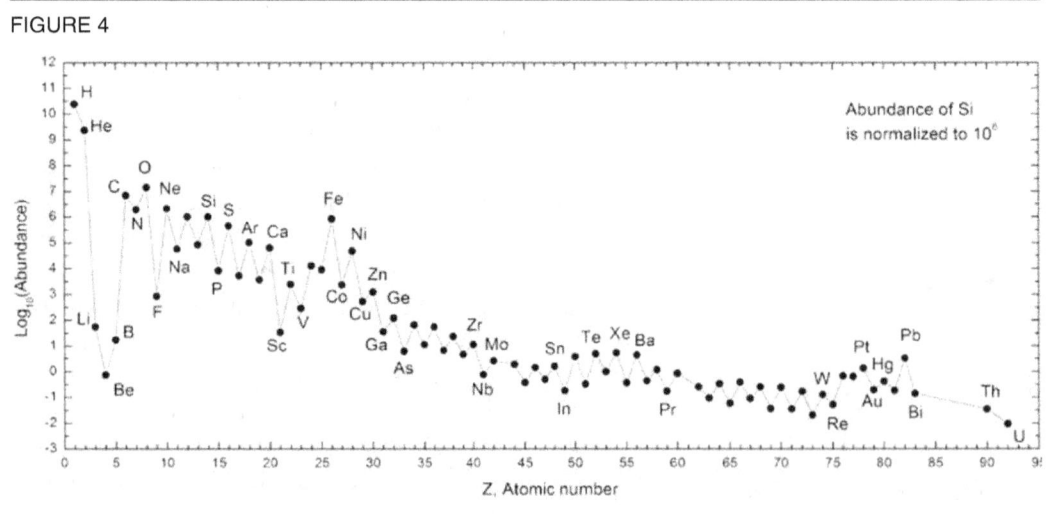

Approximate abundance of elements in the Solar System.

wikipedia user 28 bytes

of evidence is even more difficult to explain: the processes broadly categorized as low-energy nuclear reactions. We learn about this by doing experiments in which palladium (or nickel-palladium) electrodes are immersed in heavy water (water with deuterium replacing normal hydrogen). In the experiments, an electric current is used to help the palladium lattice absorb deuterium until the lattice is saturated. The elements in the electrodes are measured before and after.

The results are astonishing. Beginning with a particular distribution of isotopes of palladium, all distributions change (**Figure 5**). Beginning with just four elements (palladium, platinum, heavy hydrogen and oxygen) many more elements emerge: transmutation at low energies.

Some of the elements are palladium or platinum plus a proton and neutron (heavy hydrogen), but others are about half of either, implying fission (**Figure 6**). No neutrons are detected, as are found in the fission of uranium or plutonium, but heat not accounted for by chemical reactions of the constituents is detected. How could a hydrogen get from the metal lattice into the palladium nucleus? Neutrons were originally used to transmute elements because neutrons, being neutral, easily penetrated the positively charged nucleus. But to cause a positively charged nucleus (like heavy hydrogen) to combine with another nucleus, it is generally believed that a much larger amount of energy, usually provided by an accelerator or very high temperatures, is required.

Could some kind of resonance phenomenon be at play here? Cook points out that low-energy nuclear reactions could be the most fruitful field for exploring the structure of the nucleus.

FIGURE 5

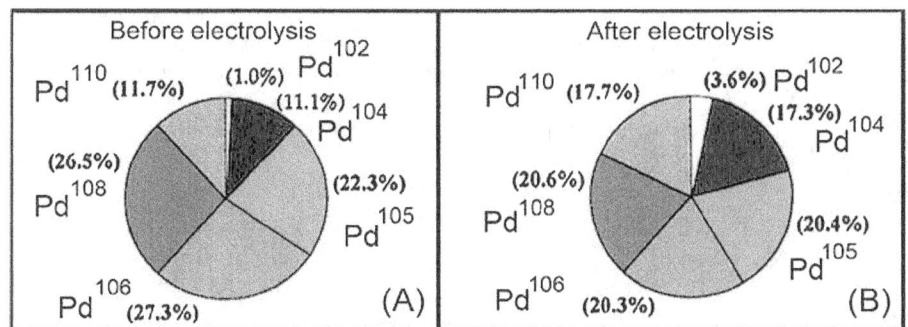

Mizuno, 1998.

Changes in palladium isotope abundance due to electrolysis.

FIGURE 6

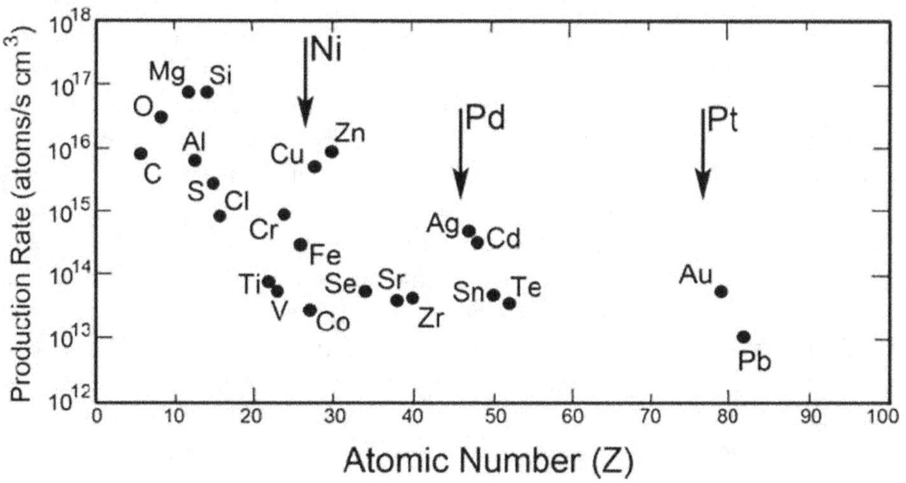

Nuclear reaction products reported by Miley and Patterson (1996) using a platinum anode and nickel-palladium cathode.

Miley and Patterson, 1996.

Other Avenues: Harmony of the World

How would a Kepler or Mendeleev approach this problem were either alive today?

Why choose one model over another, other than because the facts fit? There is at least one other well-known period of history when the models fit the data almost perfectly, and could be infinitely adjusted to accommodate observational accuracy, and yet something fundamentally wrong about the universe was being assumed. The case that comes to mind is that of Ptolemaic epicycles.

Claudius Ptolemy (ca. 100-170 AD) had the Sun and planets orbiting the stationary Earth and accounted for planets sometimes going backwards by having the planet travel on a small circle which travelled on the larger orbit. Finding that there were still differences to account for, he moved the planets' orbits off-center from the Earth. Since that still wasn't good enough, he added another point that wasn't the Earth or their orbital centers, that would control their motions.

When Nicolaus Copernicus developed his Sun-centered system, he changed the physical description, allowing the Earth to move, but added even more circles than Ptolemy had. His model matched the planets' actual positions better than did Ptolemy's, but how much was from putting the Sun in the center, and how much from adding more circles and having more observations?

Johannes Kepler's one-time employer, Tycho Brahe, developed a system in which the Sun and moon circled the stationary Earth, while the planets revolved around the moving Sun. He had fantastic observations, and his model was even better at predicting where the planets would be seen than Copernicus's. It was numerically superior, even though it was physically wrong, by our standards. Better observations, and more adjustments, make for better models.

In this way, any anomaly could have been accounted for, and more circles could always be added if necessary. But what about reality? Kepler introduced four (at least) fundamentally new, universal concepts into astronomy:

1. Kepler introduced physics. He was the first, not Copernicus, to propose that the Sun actually moved the planets, and that therefore motion must be accounted for relative to the Sun, not just around it.

2. The Universe is not based on uniform motion but instead upon constant change.

3. The parameters determining the orbits of the planets are not arbitrary, but depend on musical necessity.

4. Humans have a unique isomorphism with creation, such that they can continually come closer and closer to knowing the cause of things, and act on the basis of that knowledge. In this way, Kepler is the father of science as we know it today.

An accountant or pure mathematician perhaps might argue that numerically, Kepler only accounted for a few decimal places more of accuracy.

Dr. Robert Moon (1911-89) of the Manhattan Project had asked precisely the question I asked above. How would Kepler have approached the paradoxes posed by the nucleus? From this he offered what is now known as the Moon Model of the nucleus, which constructs the various nuclei from embedded Platonic solids. Dr. Moon also had a hypothesis that the nuclear decay, generally considered a stochastic process (random with some direction), may in fact be due to forces we have not yet investigated, perhaps in the very

FIGURE 7

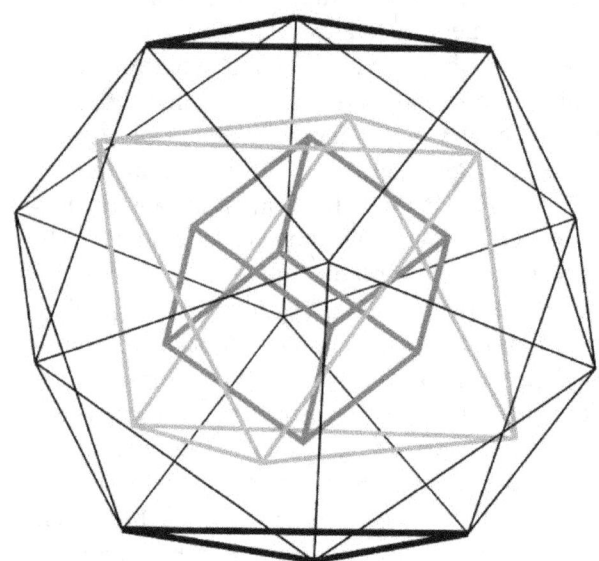

Embedding of Platonic solids used by Dr. Robert Moon to model the atomic nucleus. The Platonic solids are the only regular polyhedra that exist, an indication of the topology of space. Kepler used an embedding of Platonic solids to approximate the distances of the planets known to him. The closure of each solid are at oxygen, silicon, iron, and palladium. Dr. Moon uses two of these structures to account for nuclei up to uranium.

large, such as cosmological processes.

This hypothesis was partially confirmed by the work of Dr. Simon Shnoll (1930-), who showed with meticulous measurements, that the fine structure of atomic decay, previously considered to be totally random (stochastic), revealed periodicities that correspond to daily, lunar, solar and other cycles.[1]

Shnoll also looked at a domain which is very lightly touched, namely life. He first saw these variations in life processes as a chronobiologist. There is some evidence, though sparse, that life discerns nuclear differences with a finer-toothed comb than non-life processes, and not just based on mass differences. There is some even more sparse evidence that life might transmute elements. Just as life processes are very picky about the handedness of their molecules, which are chemically indistinct, could there be a nuclear graininess which life recognizes, that is not accounted for in physics?

Surprise! We don't know everything! What new physical principles await, which, provoked by the paradoxes in the very small, will tell us something about how the Universe is fundamentally organized?

---

1. Simon Shnoll, *Cosmophysical Factors in Stochastic Processes*, (American Research Press, 2009).

Iran's Contributions to World Fusion Research Poised for Take-Off

by Marsha Freeman

Sept. 5—The July 14 nuclear agreement between Iran and the P5+1 nations of China, France, Germany, Russia, the United Kingdom, and the United States will remove sanctions and other barriers, and create the opportunity to fully integrate scientists in Iran into global scientific research. One field of research that is specifically mentioned in the agreement, is the great challenge of all of humanity—nuclear fusion energy. Iran's direct participation in the front-line International Thermonuclear Experimental Reactor (ITER), which is under construction in France, is noted in the agreement as a possibility.

Dr. Mahmood Ghoranneviss

program's accomplishments, and point to the pathways for cooperation in the future.

Dr. Mahmood Ghoranneviss is Dean of the Plasma Physics Research Center of the Science & Research Branch of the Islamic Azad University, located northwest of Tehran. In 1994, Dr. Ghoranneviss inaugurated the Research Center and since then, has led the fusion research program in Iran. The Center is the most advanced of its kind in Iran, in plasma physics, training, and research and development in nuclear fusion.

Dr. Ghoranneviss is also Director of the *Journal of Theoretical and Applied Physics*, associated with Azad University. The Journal is open and free of charge to all readers and authors. He has published in, and been guest editor of, a number of international scientific journals. He is the author of 28 books, holds patents in Germany and the United States, and has contributed to 334 scientific papers.

The contributions that Iran has made to move fusion research forward remain unrecognized even among most members of the world's scientific community. It is critical now to mobilize all of the world's scientific resources to bring about the transition to a fusion-based world economy.

Iran has a vibrant and growing fusion energy research program, which includes various approaches to fusion, and many fields of applications of plasma technology. Reaching the goal of developing fusion technology for large-scale energy production, fusion scientists agree, is greatly enhanced by international cooperation.

Over the past month, Iranian fusion scientist Dr. Mahmood Ghoranneviss has provided answers to questions about Iran's fusion research program, posed to him via email by *EIR* Technology Editor, Marsha Freeman. Dr. Ghoranneviss has provided the photographs of Iran's IR-T1 Tokamak, which help to illustrate the

EIR: Dr. Ghoranneviss, please tell us about your background, and major areas of research.

Ghoranneviss: I earned my Bachelor of Science from Tehran University, Iran, in 1977, a Master of Science in 1980, and doctoral degree in plasma physics in 1988, from Poona University in India.

I began my research at the Atomic Energy Organization of Iran in the Plasma Physics Research Group in 1983, and a decade later, in 1993, founded the Plasma Physics Research Center. I have developed and equipped 12 advanced physics laboratories for research in a variety of areas. These have included fusion approaches such as the plasma focus and inertial confinement fusion, and applications such as chemical vapor deposition, the plasma torch, the low-temperature plasma jet, and low-power lasers. My main area of research has been in magnetic confinement fusion, and I also developed industrial and medical applications of plasmas.

EIR: Iran, it is well known, is an oil-rich country. Why, then, is Iran pursuing a fusion energy program?

Plasma Physics Research Center/Islamic Azad University

Iran's IR-T1 tokamak is contributing to global fusion research under the small tokamaks program of the International Atomic Energy Agency. Here, an aerial view.

Ghoranneviss: Since Iran's resources are not permanent, we need to look for new energy sources, such as fusion energy. Iran's plan is to have clean fusion power for the future.

EIR: What are the main magnetic fusion experiments in Iran?

Ghoranneviss: The IR-T1 tokamak, which focuses on the development of diagnostics, and the study of MHD [magnetohydrodynamic] instabilities in plasmas. In 1994, the IR-T1 tokamak was purchased from China. The machine stands 2.5 meters tall, with a weight of 2.7 tons, and a radius of the toroidal chamber of 45 centimeters. Since 2006, there is also a Plasma Focus Laboratory at the Center, which houses three devices, which are homemade.

EIR: I understand Iran participates in international fusion research with the IR-T1 tokamak. How does this research contribute to the international ITER tokamak program?

Ghoranneviss: The ITER project is facing many challenges. In order to solve the problems of fusion, small tokamaks in different countries are used, because working with a small tokamak is much easier, and is affordable. IR-T1 focuses on diagnostic plasma parameter mesurements, and MHD instabilities, which are important for ITER.

Since 2006, we have had two contracts with the IAEA [International Atomic Energy Agency of the United Nations] to carry out research which supports ITER. These contracts are under the Coordinated Research Project of the IAEA, which supports joint research using small tokamaks, for theoretical and experimental studies that can be applied to ITER.

EIR: I would think that Iran's participation in internatioal fusion research has been affected by the Western sanctions. Is this the case?

Ghoranneviss: Yes. During these years, we faced so many problens due to the sanctions. Most of the time, we could not attend the important conferences, due to visa rejections. (In my case, I applied for a U.S. visa, but my visa got rejected). In some cases, we could get a visa, with much difficulty, but then during the conference and laboratory tours, conference organizers did not let us visit their labs and setups. Another problem is in buying the things that we need for our

Diagnostic instruments inserted inside the tokamak provide scientific measurements of plasma parameters and behavior.

center from developed countries, such as material, setup, and measurement systems: They simply don't sell to us! Some journals also do not publish papers from our country.

EIR: How many people are working in plasma physics and fusion research in Iran?

Ghoranneviss: We have about 100 scientists who are working on fusion research in Iran, and there are more than 150 PhD students working on plasma and fusion topics. More than 150 papers from our University have been published by our graduate students in fusion.

In total, there are more than 1,200 students at our Center, including 800 undergraduate students, in laser physics, plasma physics, soild state physics, and 200 Masters of Science students in comparable fields.

On August 22, I reported that the Plasma Physics Research Center is recruiting postdoctoral researchers in fusion energy and plasma technology. This program

Ten Years of Progress

The Iranian program has accomplished the following disagnostic up-grades to its IR-T1 Tokamak over the decade 2005-2015.

1. Installation of a new data acquisition system with 144 channels
2. Timing and triggering systems have been upgraded
3. Upgrading of 42-channels amplifier to amplify signals from the IR-T1 Tokamak
4. Design and fabrication of 40 channels integrator with time constant (1ms, 4ms, 10ms)
5. Design and calibration of 3 high-precision rogowski coils to measure the main fields of the IR-T1 Tokamak
6. Replacement of all vacuum systems according to the latest standard
7. Design and fabrication of limiter bias system for impressment of the bias voltage to plasma in the IR-T1 Tokamak
8. Installation of a high-purity hydrogen generator
9. Design and construction of a Feedback system to control the horizontal displacement of plasma in the IR-T1 Tokamak
10. Improvement of all high voltage relays
11. Design and fabrication of a movable Langmuir probe
12. Maintenance of resonance helical field (RHF) system in IR-T1 Tokamak
13. Design and fabrication of 16-channels Rack probe
14. Design and fabrication of a Movable limiter
15. Design and fabrication of Mach probe to measure plasma radial speed in IR-T1 Tokamak
16. Installation of Reseal Gas Analyzer (RGA)
17. Design and fabrication of Ball pen probe.

is being supported by the Iran National Science Foundation.

One of our current projects is to design and fabricate a superconducting tokamak, as a national project.

EIR: Could you describe your Center's research work with the plasma focus? This is a very promising approach to fusion, and is being studied with more advanced fusion fuels, to produce aneutronic reactions, that is, without producing damaging neutrons. It has also involved some interesting international collaboration.

Ghoranneviss: The Plasma Focus Laboratory at the Center was established in 2006, and includes research and development, and the training of manpower. In research on the plasma focus, we have projects with the United States, China, and Australia.

We have been collaborating with Lawrenceville Plasma Physics (LPP) in New Jersey, on plasma focus research, under a contract signed in 2012. The two laboratories agreed to collaborate in the publication of scientific papers, exchange of ideas for plasma focus designs, share the results of research and simulations,

and the joint supervision of PhD student theses.

We are still taking our first steps, and have not published any results yet, but we are designing, and now fabricating the set-up for the experiments.

EIR: You have developed some very interesting applications drawn from fusion research, using low-temperature plasmas, electron beams, and other spin-offs. Can you describe these?

Ghoannevis: We have designed and built two electron beam systems, which can be applied to lithography in the microelectronics industry; in the food industry, for packaging products; in welding, melting, and evaporating materials; as well as the sterilization of medical equipment.

We have developed applications for plasmas in medicine. This is a relative newcomer to this field. We have developed a "Plasma Needle," that uses a low-temperature and low-power plasma. This plasma can be used for sterilization, disinfection, in dentistry, and other applications. Plasma medicine is rapidly developing. We have already started much experimental research in this new field.

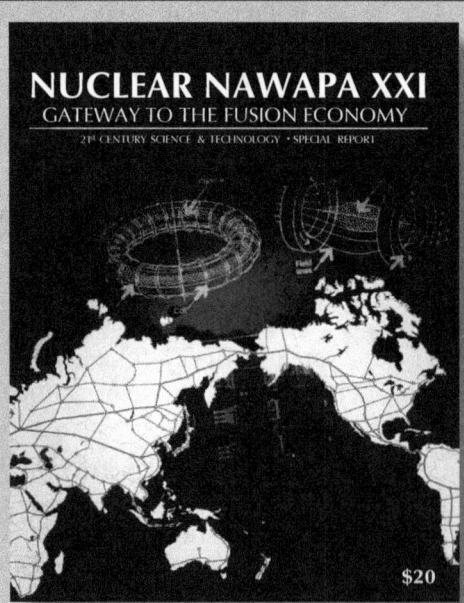

The Role of Wilhelm Furtwängler In the New Paradigm for Peace: The New Eurasian Landbridge

by Mindy Pechenuk with Megan Beets

But, at the end of this week and the beginning of next week, one of the most momentous developments in all modern history is about to unfold. It's going to unfold underneath this new assembly of the international movement of peace, which is the best term to call it. And so from that point on, we have to realize that that's the case. We are at the threshold of thermonuclear war. . . .

Lyndon LaRouche
Schiller Institute Conference
New York City, September 12, 2015

Wilhelm Furtwängler conducts the New York Philharmonic at Carnegie Hall in 1925.

The creative universal principle which is generative throughout our universe is a dynamic of *physical space-time*, not that of the commonly understood and dominating popular idea of *clock-time*. Even as this article is being written, the universe we live in has been undergoing fundamental changes due to that creative principle, which we cannot see with our senses. It is this same creative process which governs our mind, and it is only mankind's mind (no animal has this capability) which has the power to transform our universe, our galaxy, and our society in a principled upward development. The creative human mind has the capacity to create, from living in the future, new developments of both culture and science, which develop new relations among people and nations—a new paradigm of peace.

By the time you read this article, many more momentous developments will have happened, transformed by the highly-successful Schiller Institute Conference in New York City on September 12, 2015[1]: the press conference of former Senator Mike Gravel at the United Nations on Monday, September 14, 2015[2]; and the organizing of the U.S. population by the LaRouche PAC, centered in Manhattan; as well as the crucial roles that President Putin, President Xi Jinping, and other international friends are playing, as in the case of Germany today.

Both President Putin and President Xi Jinping have made offers to the United States to join this new development for peace; and both the LaRouche PAC led by Lyndon LaRouche, and the Schiller Institute led by

---

1. See the video of the September 12, 2015 Schiller Institute Conference: "Creating A Peace Paradigm, A New Era For Mankind Where We All Become Truly Human".
2. Video and audio of Sen. Mike Gravel speaking to UN correspondents, Monday, September 14, 2015.

Helga Zepp-LaRouche, have reached out to the people of the United States to join this new paradigm of peace. *This is our last chance, and at the same time, the moment of greatest potential to succeed*, so the challenge to all the readers of this article is to find the quality of thinking of a truly human identity in yourself, which will allow you to find the courage to fight *now*; to make sure that our immortal species goes forward, and is not exterminated in the British Empire/President Obama-led thermonuclear war! We must continue to create removal of Obama with the power of the 25th Amendment.

The Case of Wilhelm Furtwängler (1886-1954): The Bridge from Brahms to Today

The crimes unleashed by the British Empire at the beginning of the Twentieth Century, are the cause of the mess which mankind finds itself in today. In the realm of music, this took the form of the horrors of irrationalism, sensuality, and the mathematical mind in so-called musical composers. At the same time, many orchestral conductors reduced conducting to the twin evils of *literal* or *sensual* interpretations of the score. In science and general education, the British Empire unleashed the satanic Bertrand Russell, whose imprisoning of physical science within the shackles of mathematics and logic has held back scientific breakthroughs up to the present day.[3]

This is the condition of the world that Furtwängler took on beginning from his early years, up until his death in 1954. As will be seen in the passages from his writings below, Furtwängler was firm in his understanding of the governing universal principle of the *future*, and that acts of creation, whether in science or art, are living, organic wholes—not built up piecemeal part by part, or note by note. Accordingly, Furtwängler's approach to a musical composition was never in the *notes*, but, what he called "between the notes." This is what separated him from the cult of popular conducting, typified by such as Arturo Toscanini, who believed in strict, literal reading of the notes. Toscanini was not alone; you can include Bruno Walter, Herbert von Karajan, and many others who hated Furtwängler for setting the universal standard, by the power of his performances, that music was not in the notes.

3. See Jason Ross, "The Failures (and Evil) of Logic: A Particularly Evil Aspect Of Bertrand Russell," EIR, April 4, 2014.

I ask you: Did you ever see a note *compose*? To believe that music is a predetermined series of relationships, or non-relationships—a collection or succession of notes—is like believing that money makes money, and that that is called economy. Did you ever see a dollar bill create a discovery?

Every time Furtwängler conducted, he rediscovered the discovery of the creative passion of the composers. When he performed Beethoven's Ninth Symphony, he knew that the subject for both Beethoven and Friedrich Schiller (whose beautiful poetry was set by Beethoven in the fourth movement "Ode to Joy") was to bring about a world in which brother could love brother, across all nations. In the hands of Furtwängler, the soul of Beethoven's mind and genius is brought alive to create a new culture for mankind.

Take what he wrote in an essay on Beethoven from 1918:

> Not only is this tempestuous Titan also the source of the profoundest, most blissful serenity of the profoundest spiritual experience, most inspiring sense of peace and harmony that has ever been conveyed in music. In the midst of the tempest, held in the grip of a raging passion, he retains his steely control, his singularity of purpose, his unshakeable determination to shape and master his material down to the very last detail with a self-discipline unparalleled in the history of art....
>
> More than any other composer he seeks to uncover the laws of nature, the eternal verities— hence the extraordinary clarity of his music. The simplicity that dominates his work is not that of a naive or primitive artist, nor does it aim at achieving an immediate sensory effect, like modern popular music. Yet no music makes its approach to the listener so directly, so openly— so nakedly, one might dare to say.

In an essay entitled "Thoughts for All Seasons," Furtwängler expresses in words the principle he knows so intimately in musical performance, and of which people like Toscanini remained entirely ignorant:

> Let us consider the activity of artistic creation. One might fairly describe it as a struggle. The conflicts that provoke this struggle have their roots in the substance, the material (in the broad-

est sense) of the art in question—its forms, colors, harmonies and so on. The artist's task is to harness the forces inherent in this substance to a single common purpose.

When we look more closely at this process, we find we can distinguish two levels. On the first, each individual element combines with those adjacent to it to form larger elements, these larger elements then combining with others and so on, a logical outwards growth from the part to the whole. On the other level, the situation is the reverse: the given unity of the whole controls the behavior of the individual elements within it, down to the smallest detail. The essential thing to observe is that in any genuine work of art these two levels complement each other, so that the one only becomes effective when put together with the other.

In another essay discussing the genius of J.S. Bach, Furtwängler again elaborates the principle of the absolute coherence and unity of the moment "in time," and the whole "above time":

> [In Bach] we find concentration on the moment in time united with the unheard expanse; the immediate realization of the part paired with the truly sovereign overall vision of the whole. With its ever-conscious feeling for the near and the far at the same time; with its unconstrained fulfillment of the here-and-now joined with an ever-present subconscious feeling for the structure, the current of the whole; its 'near-experience' (*Nah-Erleben*) with its 'distance-hearing' (*Fernhören*), Bach's music is a greater example of biological certainty of purpose and natural power than we will find anywhere else in Music. Precisely this is what makes Bach's music so truly unique....

Furtwängler to America (1925-1927): The Battle for Our Soul

Upon arriving in the United States, Furtwängler was an immediate success. His first performance at New York City's Carnegie Hall on January 3, 1925 sparked a ferment which stretched to his last performance in New York in 1927, and it was warfare all the way through with the British Empire agents in New York City. They

U.S. Office of War Information
Furtwängler's opponent Arturo Toscanini, in 1944.

had another agenda: to control Alexander Hamilton's New York, and the rest of the United States, and to deliver it back into the hands of Wall Street and the Confederacy. The policy of these British Empire-allied forces was to bring in the literalist, mechanical Arthur Toscanini to replace Furtwängler.[4]

Even while Furtwängler was in New York for the first time, conducting the New York Philharmonic in January of 1925, Clarence H. Mackay and the Philharmonic Board were making plans to bring in Toscanini, which plan was announced in June of that year. Appropriately, the lead music critic for the *New York Times* wrote the following for the occasion:

> If ever there was a man who justified the theory of aristocracy built upon the fundamental conception that men are not born free and equal, that some are immeasurably superior to others, and that their superiority is justification for their con-

---

4. I want to put in a note of caution, from this point on, that when I name certain individuals, I am doing so from the standard that Lyndon LaRouche raised at the September 12, 2015 Schiller Institute Conference: "You see it on people who don't know that they are evil, and doing evil things. They have evil ideas; their religious beliefs, or similar things. No, the corruption is *not* the individuals. The corruption lies in the process. That's been the history. And our history of the United States, particularly with Alexander Hamilton's study, and what he did, as opposed to what his opponents did. And that's the real story.

"The idea that there are particular bad people running loose, Yes, I know about the mafia. They're bad people. I know that. But that's not,— the mafia is *not* the instrument of evil. It is merely the errand boys of local evil. So, the issues have to go deeper. They go to matters of principle, not to gossip."

trol of others' acts and destinies, that man is Arturo Toscanini. Outside of his art we need not question or discuss him, nor make a matter for academic argument the question of the attitude of the individual toward his fellows. In that sphere, which is the freest and highest playground for the human spirit, he stands as a hero and a master; one who has never yielded an inch to self-interest or expediency; who is completely and unmistakably contemptuous of such matters as public praise or financial gain, and who has kept the flame of his art through every fact of existence clear and bright and intense. It is with something more than the curiosity that awaits the appearance of a famous guest conductor that the Philharmonic audiences will gather to meet Mr. Toscanini.[5]

This warfare continued throughout 1925-27 (the latter the year of Furtwängler's third and last trip to America), and was run primarily via British Empire-directed operations involving department store executive and State Department agent Ira Hirschmann. Ira Hirschmann became the upfront "do it" person for this policy. He set up one of the first radio stations to bring Classical music to the American people, WOR-710 AM, and naturally only allowed the American people to hear his favorites: "Bruno Walter, Otto Klemperer and my special hero, Maestro Arturo Toscanini."[6] It is no accident that their so-called "educational policy" never played Furtwängler for the population at large!

Unknown to most Americans today, there were the fortunate Americans who *did* hear Furtwängler during his concert tours, and who were not able to be silenced about his not being granted the conductorship of the New York Philharmonic:

The fact that Mr. Furtwängler is not returning next season has little or nothing to do with his ability or his obvious popularity with his audiences, and with the all too little considered minority—the Philharmonic Orchestra. Why, then, are we about to lose the services of this man who is surely one of the world's greatest conductors and is appreciated as such in every musical community but this? ... Among the Philharmonic directors, who we must admire for their sacrifice of time and money to art, there are not those in

any way qualified to pass judgment on the musical qualities of a great composer, a great conductor, or a great soloist. Their judgment of artists is largely influenced by the latter's capability of producing the sensational. Art is the outcome of sincerity, understanding and repose. Sensationalism is an artificial hypodermic....[7]

Another American patriot fighting for the soul of America also wrote to the *New York Times*:

Is there a conspiracy against Wilhelm Furtwängler? ... Why all of a sudden, when Toscanini conducts, forget everyone, and knock Furtwängler especially? It isn't fair play, and it is with profound regret that I look upon the absence of this sincere artist who consistently refuses to prostitute his art for applause and the favor of critics.[8]

Now let the music speak for itself.

The reader should access the following two examples of performances of the second movement, the "Funeral March," of Beethoven's 3rd Symphony ("Eroica"). The first is a performance of the Vienna Philharmonic conducted by Furtwängler in December of 1944, a time when Furtwängler was becoming increasingly clear that he was going to have leave Germany, as the madman Hitler, sitting in his bunker, had put Furtwängler on his hit list.[9]

• The second movement, the "Funeral March" of Beethoven's 3rd Symphony ("Eroica")

• A 1953 performance, conducted by Toscanini, of the NBC Symphony Orchestra (an orchestra created in 1937 specifically to bring Toscanini into New York City).

Think about what each of the two different performances of the same composition do to your mind and soul.

As Furtwängler himself wrote in his notebooks in 1936[10]:

Modern conducting: originating in the audience's instinct for actors and virtuosos, but above all its slave instinct. The authority of a Toscanini, say, could be contrasted with the truly

5. Daniel Gillis, *Furtwängler and America*, pp. 14-18.
6. Ira Hirschmann, *Obligato*, pp. 5-9.

7. Gillis, *op. cit*, p. 20.
8. Sam H. Shirakawa, *The Devil's Music Master*, p. 84.
9. Renée Sigerson, "Furtwängler: The Baton Raised to Silence Tyranny," *EIR*, August 28, 2015.
10. Wilhelm Furtwängler, *Notebooks, 1924-54*," translated by Shaun Whiteside, Quartet Books, 1995, p. 83.

natural authority of the piece! Truthfulness can only be attained through the soul. And one might say: truthfulness is the first and the most beautiful sign of noble humanity.

Again, in his notebooks of 1940, Furtwängler writes[11]:

Universal things can only be said in a universal language. Because this language is universal, because the things to be said in it are meant to be universal, it does not follow that they must have appeared before. The mark of all truly great work, whether that of yesterday or tomorrow, is that it is both old and new, that it has never existed before and yet one has the feeling of having known it for ages. But everything else, everything that does not in its own way strive for universality, is subjectivism, and *only* this is subjectivism. Which is, today, as it always has been and always will be—superficial.

Here are two conflicting worldviews: that of Furtwängler, who truly lives and creates from the true human identity, as he would say, "between the notes," where the soul and mind unite with the higher principle of creation. Between the notes—where great paradoxes occur which have no *literal* rendering, but only a higher order resolution, creating a new *gestalt* or discovery.

On the other hand, there is that of Toscanini, and the others like him, who carry the banner for the deconstruction of the human mind and soul. This is why Toscanini was brought into New York against Furtwängler by the British Empire and its satanic helpers, like the *New York Times* and people such as Olin Downs, Clarence Mackay, and Ira Hirschmann, to name a few. Toscanini's conducting could make the notes play in time, but he could not create real Classical music.

Furtwängler makes this clear with the visit of Toscanini to Germany. He writes in his notebook of 1930[12] where he stands concerning Toscanini's performance of

Encounter magazine was the organ for the post-war Congress for Cultural Freedom, which was determined to crush the Classical idea represented by the likes of Furtwängler.

11. Furtwängler, *op. cit.*, p. 123.
12. Furtwängler, *op. cit.*, pp. 44-45.

Beethoven's Eroica Symphony that year in Germany:

…The exaggeratedly sluggish tempo of the death-march—what about literalness?—could also be explained by peculiar needs. The march-like aspect was completely unrecognizable even in the realistic first bars, and Beethoven's gloomy, tearless and wordless mourning is dissolved into beautiful-sounding sentimentality.…

The World After the Death of President Franklin Delano Roosevelt

Unfortunately for humanity, the great President Franklin Roosevelt died in 1945. Had he lived, the British Empire would have been defeated then, in the period after World War II, and the millions of human lives that have been lost since, those many generations of precious human souls, would have been able to contribute to the future of humanity.

Lyndon LaRouche has often spoken to us of this moment in history, when he was a young soldier in World War II, stationed in the India-Burma theater. The night President Roosevelt died, the young men who were serving with Lyndon asked him to meet with them, and asked him what he thought about the death of President Roosevelt, and the new President Truman. Lyndon LaRouche's prescient voice was clear: "We have lost a great President, and now we have a little man."

The Presidency of Harry S Truman ushered in an era of the destruction of our nation and mankind. This destruction has only been furthered by fifteen years of the presidencies of the Bush family, and now Obama.

Under the British Empire agent Harry S Truman, hell was unleashed in the United States. Witch hunts were begun through FBI director J. Edgar Hoover, his assets such as Roy Cohn, General Robert McClure, State Department agents (as in the case of Ira Hirschmann), and the whole project of the Congress of Cultural Freedom, which interfaced many CIA and British Intelligence capabilities. Like FDR, and La-

Rouche today, Furtwängler was subject to many of these operations. In the case of Furtwängler, they branded him a Nazi, and forced him to go through the de-nazification process. To be blunt, the British Empire and everyone else involved knew full well that Furtwängler was not a Nazi, and that he stayed in his country, Germany, to *defend it against Hitler*.[13] However, the accusation against him was used to keep Furtwängler away from the American population, and the world.

13. For more details on the attacks against Furtwängler see Renée Sigerson, Daniel Gillis, and Sam Shirakawa, *op. cit.*

Furtwängler's Nemesis Supported Bertrand Russell

Ira Hirschmann was the decisive vote on Bertrand Russell's appointment as special guest lecturer at the New York City College System at Hunter College.

"Immediately after Russell had announced his acceptance of the school's invitation, the Board was besieged by protests. . . . As the latest appointee to the board, my turn came last. Keeping count of the yeas and nays, I knew the vote was going to be close, but I had not expected to find myself in the un-enviable position of facing a tie. Mine was to be the deciding vote.

. . . Before my turn to vote came up, I had written out a statement on the reason for my decision. . . . This is a reasonably close recollection:

The issue here is not Bertrand Russell, but academic freedom. Too little respect for this hallmark of our democratic process, so hard won, has been manifested in recent times in our country. It is being flouted in Germany. My convictions on this subject are strong and unequivocal. I vote 'Yes.'"[1]

While Ira Hirschmann, the spokesman for the policy of the British Empire, tried to thrust the evil of Bertrand Russell on the future minds of our nation, at the same time that he was running every possible operation he could to destroy and silence the genius of Wilhelm Furtwängler.

Fortunately, in spite of Ira Hirschmann's vote, the people of New York City spoke out, and the appointment of Bertrand Russell was revoked.

1. Ira Hirschmann, *Caution to the Wind*, pp. 120-122.

Furtwängler vs. the Congress for Cultural Freedom

Throughout the end of the 1940s into the 1950s, the intensity of the cultural battle for the soul of mankind was escalated by many different factions, all under the skirts of the British Empire. There was the CIA-funded Congress for Cultural Freedom,[14] the operations run by the crowd around Ira Hirschmann; and there were other conductors of evil who were promoted instead of Furtwängler, such as von Karajan (who *was* a card-carrying Nazi) and Bruno Walter (who also led attacks against Furtwängler).

For our purposes in this short article, I will highlight the fight around Furtwängler's proposed appointment to the Chicago Symphony in 1948. Furtwängler's own statement from his Notebook in 1949 makes the issue quite clear:

. . . A number of celebrated American artists have protested at my proposed visit to America. They do not even want me to be allowed to stay there for a few weeks as a guest. This protest by artists against another artist is something completely new, a monstrosity in the history of music, a slap in the face to all previous concepts of ideal solidarity among artists, of the function of art in uniting peoples and serving the cause of peace. They have acted in a personal way against me, so I too shall become somewhat personal.

At the head of list I see the illustrious name of A. Toscanini. What can have caused him, the great man, who stands above oppositions, to take part in this short-sighted and ill-founded protest? Was he not the one who, in 1936, invited me to New York as his successor, and a few months later in Paris hurled reproaches at me for not accepting this post despite overwhelming opposition? And at that time it had long been clear that despite resigning from my official posts I would remain in Germany. Certainly he suddenly said a year later, when I successfully conducted along with him in Salzburg, that one could not perform Beethoven in an oppressed and a free country at the same time, while I was of the opinion that Beethoven makes his audiences 'free' wherever

14. See: "Children of Satan III: The Sexual Congress for Cultural Fascism."

he is played. But what is the reason for his refusal to let me conduct today, in free and democratic America? Four years after the war? I am faced with a puzzle! There is also Arthur Rubinstein, whom I do not know, but who plainly does not know me either, for he should know that I was the one artist who remained in Germany and emphatically intervened on behalf of Jews until the very end. Then I see Herr Brailowsky and Herr Isaac Stern. Have these two not condescended to play, in the past year, at the celebration concerts in Lucerne, although they must have known that I am definitively employed here as a conductor? Then I see my old friend Gregor Piatigorsky, the long-haired solo cellist of the Berlin Philharmonic. I watched the beginnings of his rise with my own eyes, and even shortly before the war, when it had been long clear that I was staying in Germany, we associated in a most friendly manner in Paris.

When they are in Europe, do they have a different conscience from the one they have in America, which permits them to do in Lucerne what they have to refuse in Chicago?

What is the reason for all this? The whole thing is organized. This is a boycott which has been introduced with a particular aim in mind. Individuals, I have been told, received anonymous telephone calls threatening to make their lives in America 'impossible' if they did not take part in the Furtwängler boycott. And this also explains why the refusals of all the conductors and soloists invited by the orchestra in Chicago all arrived on the same day. The orchestra was simply placed in a difficult position.

If one considers that this boycott is based entirely on accusations which were thoroughly refuted in a one-and-a-half-year trial against me, which was certainly not organized and carried out by my friends, one involuntarily wonders: So what are the *real* reasons for this trial, for this kangaroo court, this calumny against an artist respected in the whole rest of the world? Might it have something to do with my being a German? Is it not the task of art and artists to unite peoples and serve peace, not to perpetuate hatred yet again, four years after the end of the war?

I shall save myself the answer.[15]

---

15. Furtwängler, *op. cit.*, pp. 190-191.

The Call to the Future

On Saturday, September 12, 2015, Helga Zepp-LaRouche extended the hand of Furtwängler when she called on the American population to become more creative and more active, to make this moment in history live up to the creative process that Furtwängler, Schiller, Beethoven, Bach, Brahms, Einstein, Riemann and others before us had made in their contributions to the future of humanity!

At that meeting in New York, Helga sounded the trumpet to all of us:

So, what I'm really doing is I'm calling upon you to become even more active than you are already. We have the United Nations General Assembly, and I wrote an appeal to this effect, and in my view, maybe, and Lyn said the same thing, *it may really be the last chance for humanity to change course.*

...Enough is enough! We want the United States to join with these countries to build the world, and stop wars based on lies and support of terrorists, one organization after the other!

And I think if we get enough motion of people who say, it is really time for the United States to be a republic again, and not try to be an empire, and have a unipolar world, based on the Project for a New American Century, which is really what is at work here still; that the United States will not allow any country or a number of countries to come up and be superior or even equal, that policy has to stop! The United States must accept they are not the only superpower anymore.

This is the time to end hate, and take the lesson from the lives and work of the great conductor Wilhelm Furtwängler, and Helga and Lyndon LaRouche. Let us be each other's brother, and take this moment to remove Obama with the powers of the 25th Amendment, and open the door to bring all of humanity into the higher powers of the creative mind. I believe this is what Furtwängler had in mind when he conducted the most extraordinary performance of his life, in 1951, a performance of Schubert's Ninth Symphony. Let us today grab the baton from Furtwängler and answer the call to create the most incredible breakthrough, that expresses true humanity!